# GROWING UP
## WITH THE WILD BUNCH

# GROWING UP
# WITH THE WILD BUNCH
*The Story of Pioneer Legend Josie Bassett*

## LINDA WOMMACK

# TWODOT®

GUILFORD, CONNECTICUT
HELENA, MONTANA

# A · TWODOT® · BOOK

An imprint of The Rowman & Littlefield Publishing Group, Inc.
4501 Forbes Blvd., Ste. 200
Lanham, MD 20706
www.rowman.com
A registered trademark of The Rowman & Littlefield Publishing Group, Inc.

Distributed by NATIONAL BOOK NETWORK

British Library Cataloguing in Publication Information available

**Library of Congress Control Number: 2019953877**

ISBN 978-1-4930-4715-4 (hardcover)
ISBN 978-1-4930-4716-1 (e-book)

∞™ The paper used in this publication meets the minimum requirements of American National Standard for Information Sciences—Permanence of Paper for Printed Library Materials, ANSI/NISO Z39.48-1992.

# Contents

# Acknowledgments

July 1960 and again in July 1961, Josephine Bassett McKnight Ranney Williams Wells Morris gave interviews to Mr. Murl Messersmith. I am indebted to the Dinosaur National Monument in Jensen, Utah, where the tapes are archived. My thanks also go to the Museum of Northwest Colorado in Craig, Colorado, where the typewritten transcripts are available. Not long before her death in 1964, Josie was also interviewed by the esteemed regional historian John Rolfe Burroughs. These interviews, Josie's own words, provide the structure for this work, the first full-length biography written about her.

I further consulted Burroughs's excellent history of Browns Park, *Where the Old West Stayed Young*, as well as *One Hundred Years of Brown's Park and Diamond Mountain* by lifelong residents Dick and Daun DeJournette and Grace McClure's *The Bassett Women*. In the course of my research, I began to notice discrepancies between the historical record and Josie's accounting of dates and places. A few of these were minor and probably due to misrecollection, for Josie was ninety years old at the time of the interviews.

As my research intensified, I began uncovering evidence supporting many of Josie's accounts. The best source of court records, unpublished manuscripts, handwritten letters, historical photographs, and other related documents was the extraordinary Museum of Northwest Colorado. In an effort to clarify the story's more troubling aspects, dispel myths, and flush out the truth, I relied on my friends at the museum. Many hours were spent with the museum's director, Dan Davidson, who patiently answered my questions and pointed me in the right direction. Many more hours were spent with the assistant director, Jan Gerber, as we went through filing cabinets, boxes, and computer files gathering the needed information. What a pleasure it was when I would ask for something and, almost without exception, Jan would cheerfully reply, "Yes, we have that." Nearly all the photos in this book are credited to the museum, which has a wonderful photo collection. I will never forget my visits to the Museum of Northwest Colorado. Dan and Jan's efforts greatly enhanced this work. For additional historical photographs, I relied on the fabulous work of my friend Coi E. Drummond-Gerhig, Digital Image Collection Administrator for the Denver Public Library. Also helpful was Michelle Fuller of the Uintah County History Center in Vernal, Utah. She graciously answered questions and provided documents and photographs.

In the summer of 2014, I had the pleasure to finally meet Valentine Hoy IV. Hoy not only answered my many questions about his pioneering family, but he also provided documents, including a digital copy of his great-great uncle's unpublished memoir. In May 1920 James "Jesse" Shade Hoy completed his manuscript, entitled "History of Brown's Hole." He wrote a letter to Horace Bennett in Denver, dated August 29, 1924, in which he asked for assistance in finding a publisher. Evidently Bennett was unable or unwilling to help. Hoy was never able to get his book published. Fortunately, two hard copies of the original manuscript survive. One can be found in the archives of the Colorado History Center. The other is in the possession of Hoy IV.

Special thanks go to those who believed in this project and gave freely of their time and advice. First on that list is my husband, Frank, who gave up vacation time to take me to Dinosaur National Monument, to Josie's homestead at Cub Creek, and on a few of my many trips to Browns Park and Craig, Colorado. Throughout the research and writing process, I relied on my dear friend Connie Clayton. Her cogent comments and careful editing strengthened this work immensely. I owe her my heartfelt thanks. Finally, my sincere thanks to Josephine Bassett McKnight Ranney Williams Wells Morris. She lived an extraordinary life and did what she had to do to keep her land, displaying determination and hard work in the process. I am proud to offer Josie's story in her own words, for all to read and share.

—Linda Wommack, July 10, 2018

# INTRODUCTION

LEGEND, LORE, MYSTERY, ROMANCE, AND EVEN MURDER. THESE ARE only a few of the many controversies surrounding the life of Josephine Bassett McKnight Ranney Williams Wells Morris. Raised in the legendary outlaw area of Brown's Hole, located in the extreme northwest corner of Colorado, Josie created her own legend at an early age. Josie often told of her summer romance with Butch Cassidy, who spent time as a ranch hand at the Bassett ranch before forming America's most well-known outlaw gang, the Wild Bunch. Over the years a few writers have written that Josie believed Cassidy returned from South America; one even describes her meeting once with Cassidy following his purported return. However, these writers do not cite their sources. Josie agreed to two taped interviews, conducted by Murl Messersmith on July 18, 1960, and on July 6, 1961. In these interviews, archived at the Dinosaur National Monument in Jensen, Utah, Josie mentions Cassidy quite often and eludes to his demise.

The petite pioneer woman witnessed many criminal incidents and even murder during her years in Browns Park. Josie described in detail the hanging of John Jack "Judge" Bennett from the gate post of the Bassett ranch. Josie also recounts the murder of Valentine S. Hoy. This occurred during the manhunt for outlaws Harry Tracy and David Lant, the posse of which Josie's first husband, James "Jim" McKnight, was a member.

Murder shocked the residents of Browns Park in 1900. In a culmination of the cattle wars in the area, Madison Matthew "Matt" Rash, the fiancé of Josie's sister, Ann, was murdered at his cabin. A few months later Isom Dart, the Bassetts' ranch hand, was shot to death at his cabin on Cold Spring Mountain. Josie was among the group that buried Dart near his cabin. Josie vividly recounts the time and describes a stranger present at the event, James Hicks, as suspicious and untrustworthy. Hicks would later be proven to be none other than Tom Horn, a killer hired by the cattle barons of Browns Park. Over the course of several years, Josie married five times; two of the marriages occurred within a six-month period. When her fourth husband, Emerson "Nig" Wells, died on New Year's Eve in 1912, Josie was accused of murder by an old Browns Park

Josie Morris and her horse at Josie's cabin in Cub Creek

nemesis. Although the authorities ruled the death a result of natural causes, rumors followed Josie for years. Josie would later remark, "I drove my first husband, Jim McKnight, out of the house at the point of a gun and told him never to come back. Let's just say that some men are harder to get rid of than others."

This rugged, tough-as-nails, small-statured lady moved to a new homestead on Cub Creek in Utah, where she would struggle to survive for the next fifty years. During this time, Josie became one of the most noted frontier women in the region, gaining a reputation as one of the toughest in the West. When accused of cattle rustling, Josie hired the best lawyer and fought the charges. After two trials, the sixty-two-year-old lady was acquitted of the charges.

An exposé on Josie was featured in the January 5, 1948 issue of *Life* magazine. The article garnered much attention, and reporters flocked to Cub Creek to get Josie's story. She nearly always refused. When Murl Messersmith, of Dinosaur National Monument, visited Josie at Cub Creek on July 18, 1960, and July 6, 1961, Josie agreed to be interviewed. Through years of research and with these interviews, Josie's story in her own words was finally told.

# Chapter One

# The Formidable Years

When young Josephine Bassett arrived with her parents in Brown's Hole, a legendary outlaw hideout, she had no idea that one day she would become a legend in her own right.

The Bassett family was one of the earliest families to settle in Colorado's infamous extreme-northwestern region. Samuel Bassett and Anna Marie Scott had met in Brownville, Jefferson County, New York, and married there in January 1832. On July 31, 1834, Anna Marie gave birth to their first child, Amos Herbert. Samuel Clark Bassett II followed two years later, on June 27, 1836. The family moved to Menard County, Illinois, where the elder Bassett engaged in farming. After completing his formal education, teenage Sam left the family farm, heading west for adventure and opportunity, while Amos Herbert, known as Herb, stayed on the farm, continued his education, graduated from college, and became a teacher in the local community.

When the Civil War broke out, twenty-eight-year-old Herb Bassett volunteered for the Union Army. He was mustered in as a private on August 14, 1862, at Athens, Illinois. He was assigned to serve in Company K of the 106th Regiment of "Lincoln's Brigade." A musician, Bassett joined the regiment's band with the official title of "Drummer." In 1863, barely a year into his service, Bassett fell ill. His Army records indicate the illness only as a "debility." He was sent home for a month of rest and rehabilitation. He later returned to his regiment, in which he served admirably throughout the war.

Following the war, Major Amos Herbert Bassett was honorably discharged on July 12, 1865, at Pine Bluff, Arkansas. With his background as an educator, Bassett gained government employment, serving as collector of revenue at the port of Norfolk, Virginia. Through his government work, Bassett met and became friends with many influential people, including Judge Crawford Miller, an esteemed judge in the Virginia district.

A few years later, Bassett asked Judge Miller for permission to court his granddaughter, the lovely and vivacious Mary Eliza Chamberlain Miller. Along with her sister Hannah, Mary Eliza had been orphaned when she was young. The sisters were living with their maternal grandparents when Mary Eliza met Bassett.

Not long after the courtship began, Bassett was transferred back to Arkansas, where he continued his employment as collector of revenue. He later became clerk of the district court at Little Rock. However, Bassett's courtship with Elizabeth, as she was known, continued from a distance. The pair married in Hot Springs, Arkansas, on September 21, 1871. The groom was thirty-seven years old and the bride had just turned sixteen.

It was a marriage of opposites. While both Herb and Elizabeth were well educated, their personalities were very different. Herb was a quiet, reserved, and unassuming man, while Elizabeth was charming, outgoing, and personable, though known to have quite a temper when provoked.

After their marriage, the newlyweds lived in Hot Springs, where Herb served as clerk of the court. Three years later Elizabeth gave birth to their first child, Josephine, on January 17, 1874. A son, Samuel, named for Herb's father and brother, was born two years later. Shortly after Samuel was born, Herb's health began to suffer. He later described his ailment in an application for an Army pension:

*Was treated in Arkansas 20 years ago for liver and heart trouble—had chills and fever frequently for several years after the war over—was treated by Dr. Henry C. Baker who stated that my liver was in very bad condition—that the chills and fever that I had were very hard to control. While he was treating me I had a very hard chill which*

*threatened congestion and he advised me to leave there at once. I sold
out and came here [to Brown's Hole] in April 1878.*

Due to his poor health, and after years of coaxing by his brother
Sam, Herb finally agreed to relocate to Brown's Hole. High-spirited
and adventurous Elizabeth supported her husband's decision with great
enthusiasm.

Josephine Bassett was just four years old when her parents settled the
family in Brown's Hole, Colorado, an area spanning the borders of Utah,
Wyoming, and Colorado. Years later, Josie, as everyone called her, spoke
of the journey:

*I don't know how many days we were in coming—I just barely can
remember it. I was four years old. They had a team of oxen, and wasn't
I afraid of those oxen! Oh! But I rode with them—I rode with Uncle
Sam Bassett and his oxen all the way. But when I was on the ground
I wasn't with them, I was someplace else. We landed in Green River
City. You see, there was no roads to Browns Park [Hole] from Rock
Springs at the time. We come over the mountains to Green River City
to Browns Park [Hole] with teams and wagons. One team was oxen,
two steers. I'll never forget it in the world. I loved those cattle, but
when they were unhitched, I was afraid of them. I would run and get
upon that wagon and ride with the steers every time, you know I was
terribly scared.*

Sam Bassett, Josie's uncle, was a former scout along the Overland
Trail. He later served as a scout with Union general Nelson Miles during
the Civil War. Following the war, Bassett returned to the area of Brown's
Hole, where he filed on a homestead and became one of the area's earliest
pioneer settlers. During his travels westward Bassett kept a journal, only a
few pages of which survive. The following journal quotation was included
in the memoirs of Ann Bassett, Josie's younger sister:

*Brown's Hole, November, the month of Thanksgiving, 1852. Louis
[Simmons] and I "down in." Packs off. Mules in lush cured meadow.*

*Spanish Joe's trail for travel could be likened to an "up-state" high lane for coach-and-four. Mountains to the left of us, not in formation but highly mineralized. To the South, a range in uncontested beauty of contour, its great stone mouth drinking a river. Called on neighbors lest we jeopardize our social standing. Chief Catump, and his tribe of Utes. Male and female he created them. And Solomon in all his glory was not arrayed so fine. Beads, bones, quills, and feathers of artistic design. Buckskins tanned in exquisite coloring of amazing hues, resembling velvets of finest texture. Bows and arrows. "Let there be no strife between me and thee."*

Josie Bassett later recalled the family's arrival in Brown's Hole:

*My father and my mother and my brother Sam, he was two years younger than I, and an old man by the name of Dr. Parsons [arrived.] He's buried in Browns Park. He had the cattle you know, and of course we had to bring our household, we just needed and had to have, our bedding and grub. A hundred miles is a long ways at that time's transportation, yes it was. I thought we would never get there. Well I was terribly, terribly taken with it [the area]. I thought it was the most beautiful place I ever saw. All the hills and cattle and people on horseback. I had never been used to that. And I was quite a hand to pry into everything, what was that for, what was this for, where does this go, where did it come from? There were only a few people there, and we were the only children, two of us. My sister Ann was born in May after we got there in March.*

Ann Bassett later commented on her mother's reaction to the area: "Later when my mother glimpsed the richly green, natural meadows, and the groves of stately, wide-branched cottonwoods, she was reminded of a beautiful park in the eastern land where she was born. At once she rechristened the lovely valley, 'Browns Park.'" Elizabeth would later play an instrumental role in the 1881 renaming of Brown's Hole to Browns Park. The Bassett family initially stayed with Herb's brother Sam, as Elizabeth was in the final trimester of her pregnancy with the couple's third child. Josie described her uncle's cabin as "a funny little old log cabin with two rooms, no floors and no windows." Josie's little sister, Anna Marie, known as Ann, was born in this cabin on May 12, 1878. Josie later commented on the birth:

*My sister Ann was born in May after we got there [to] Brown's Hole] in March. She was born May 12. And I tell you, my sister was a curiosity; a baby in Browns Park. Old trappers and old mountaineers of all kinds came to see the baby. Well then, we decided to stay there. We didn't know if we lived in Utah, Wyoming or Colorado, no survey yet.*

With the help of his brother Sam, Herb Bassett built a small, five-room, single-story log home for his growing family. Herb was a man out of place in the rugged Brown's Hole frontier. A well-read, very musical scholar, he was not compatible with hard, physical, outdoor labor. On the other hand, Elizabeth, a lively Southern belle, was entirely up to the challenges of this new frontier. It wasn't long before the couple had a few head of cattle and were earning an income. Elizabeth eventually used her own money to purchase a nice herd of Durham cattle. Josie later recalled, "My father didn't know how to brand a cow—neither did she [Elizabeth], but she tried."

With Herb's ability to entertain through music and intelligent conversation, and Elizabeth's outgoing personality, the Bassett ranch became a popular place for social activity in Brown's Hole. The Bassetts made good friends there, including Judge Conway, Charlie and Mary Crouse Jarvie, Valentine Smith Hoy, and Hoy's brothers.

Years later, Josie recalled some of the early pioneers of Brown's Hole:

*We had a family by the name of Davenport. He was an Englishman. Tom Davenport was an English coal miner, didn't know his age, very fine people too, very nice people. Then we had Mr. and Mrs. Sears. They were Yankee people from Vermont, very nice people too, they had no children. And we had, oh, there's quite a lot of men in the country. Hoys came afterward.*

During the Ute Indian uprising, which culminated with the Meeker Massacre in 1879, the Bassett family and several of the area's other small-scale ranchers left Brown's Hole for their safety. When the Bassetts returned, Herb and Elizabeth were shocked to find that several head of cattle were missing. Josie described the situation:

*My father bought twenty head of heifers just before the Meeker Massacre and he branded his heifers with "U P" on the ribs. Great big "U" with the "P" connected. But while we were away in Wyoming a man came into the country, his name was Metcalf . . . and he branded with "7 U P." He had a "7" in front of our "U P" all over those cows. My father didn't know what to do, he was stranded— but my mother did. She said, "I know some of those cows, and I'm taking them." And she took them! She and Mr. Metcalf had some kind of set–with [and] she didn't use "U P" anymore, she had the cattle rebranded.*

According to Browns Park historian John Rolfe Burroughs, "Technically, 'rustling cattle' was a felony offense. It is not an exaggeration to say, however, that with very few exceptions, everybody—that is everybody among the little people (nesters, settlers, homesteaders)—in Browns Park engaged in it."

Not long after returning to the ranch, Elizabeth gave birth to her fourth child, Elbert, on June 21, 1880. Younger brother George would be born on March 29, 1884.

Now actual cattle ranchers, the Bassetts attempted to work with their fellow ranchers, including the rancher with the largest holding, Valentine S. Hoy. In 1873, Hoy drove three hundred head of cattle from Greeley, Colorado, to Brown's Hole, joining his brother, Jesse Smith Hoy. The prior year, J. S. Hoy had trailed a herd of cattle for the Crawford-Thompson Cattle Company south from Evanston, Wyoming, into the north end of Brown's Hole.

In 1884 a state survey was finally conducted. Incredible as it may seem, until then it had remained unclear exactly where in the moun-

Bassett family ranch in Browns Park, Colorado
THE MUSEUM OF NORTHWEST COLORADO-CRAIG

tainous western hills of Browns Park the Colorado state line ended and the Utah state line began. Following the survey, the state of Colorado allowed the homesteaders to file for clear title of their land. Herb Bassett immediately traveled to Hahns Peak, the seat of Routt County, to officially record his homestead on September 22, 1884. Unfortunately, other residents of Browns Park either delayed or did not officially record their land claims. In circuitous, underhanded fashion, Valentine S. Hoy also went to Hahns Peak, filing on the land that several homesteaders had not officially recorded. Hoy's undermining scheme caused outrage among the area's ranchers. Many early settlers were forced to leave, and those who remained, including Herb Bassett, never forgave the Hoy brothers for their devious treachery. Josie later recounted this episode in a taped interview:

*The Hoys came first and tried to make a monopoly of everything. In spite of it, they got a lot of men killed. V. S. Hoy wasn't a good man. He was the one [Harry] Tracy killed. You see, when the survey was made, V. S. Hoy was a smart man and all the Hoys were. He had a good head on him for business, for himself. And when this survey was made, they camped at my father's house. V. S. Hoy was cook with the survey party. He had a nice business, he was there for a purpose. He was like this little old Russian that came over to us last year, just the same. Now he knew the numbers of these places and put Swift\* on them, bought the land, and what he didn't buy with Swift, he had people coming here from Fremont, Nebraska, and Leavenworth, Kansas, and there to take up homesteads. Then he met them at Glenwood Springs, where they'd take up proof, paid them each a thousand dollars and they were gone. He had their homes and that's how the Hoys got all of the Hoy bottoms. And he tried to Swift my father's place, but my father's filing on the homestead had gone in just before his script got there, so that didn't work. My father never liked the Hoys; that made a bad spot. My dad was a very forgiving man but he never forgave that, no sir. He said, "I've been a friend to V. S. Hoy and thought he was a friend to me, and to have him do that—I'll have nothing to do with him." And he never did.*

Years later, J. S. Hoy had a decidedly different, if not arrogant, view of those early years in Browns Park:

*So far as I know, covering a period of fifty or more years, I have never known a single instance where cattlemen ever tried to or did drive an honest man or honest homesteader off the range. On the contrary,*

---

\*Josie uses the name "Swift" in describing the Hoys' underhanded land grab. It is most likely that she meant "Scrip." A man by the name of Scrip was buying up land from the government for a very cheap price once it was determined the land had not been "proven up," or the land was not legally filed in a given time frame.

*cattlemen big and little, rather invited men, poor men to live in their midst, helped them in various ways. As owners usually had plenty other work to do, and cowboys had a decided repugnance to engage in farming, they encouraged the "poor man" to homestead; gave them employment at times, such as freighting in supplies, helping make hay, bought their hay, grain and vegetables, and at times gave them beef and other provisions without charge when they were in need.*

Nevertheless, the Hoy brothers lost the respect of many citizens of Browns Park. Perhaps their disdain for Hoy's actions and the fallout of those actions can best be summarized by Josie's later remarks: "The Hoys, with family money to invest, had ambitions of setting up a range empire, but found themselves so hedged in by other outfits and belligerent homesteaders that they had to content themselves with relatively modest spreads."

As the ranch began to show a profit, the Bassetts were able to hire ranch hands, including Isom Dart, a former slave, and Madison Matthew "Matt" Rash, both of whom were former employees of the Middlesex Cattle Company, a large company that had expanded operations into Browns Park. Other hired ranch hands would later include Jack Fitch, Angus McDougall, and James "Jim" Fielding McKnight.

The Bassett ranch soon became known as a place that welcomed neighbors and strangers with no questions asked. Herb and Elizabeth may or may not have known of the outlaw element that frequented the area. Hiram "Hi" Bernard, who would later marry Ann Bassett, recalled, "The old Bassett Ranch has some time or another housed most everyone in this Park or part of the North West. [Deputy sheriff] Charley Sparks made his home there, when he first came west as a boy, from North Carolina. Sparks is a wealthy man now." The Bassetts were known throughout the Park for entertaining. Guests were treated to Elizabeth's fine cooking and Herb's musical talent. Long evenings were spent dancing on a unique wooden floor Herb had constructed. Josie later recalled:

*The old-timers came and enjoyed it. Mom would bake pies and cookies and a lot of things. We had supper, sometimes they danced on the floor. Many people didn't have floors, 'cause lumber was scarce. They had to haul lumber from Green River and times you couldn't even get a board in Green River City. I can remember when our house had had dirt floors. Father hewed a cottonwood log and made puncheons. They are just cut in half and taken green, then they are hewed smooth on each side with an old broad ax. I had the old broad ax, packed it around with me for years and years and years. I gave it to the Daughters of the Pioneers, I thought that's where it belonged.*

The Bassetts raised their children in the open atmosphere of the West. They were taught at an early age to rope, ride, and shoot. This upbringing became ingrained in all the Bassett children, as was their mother's love for Browns Park.

Josie had fond memories of her childhood. She often played in the sandy Vermilion Creek with nearby Indian children of her own age.

*I was perhaps five or six at the time, and I remember it so well. We didn't speak the same language, but we got along famously. We made little houses out of wet sand and clay, and diverted little rivulets from Vermilion Creek to make play rivers. It sounds like a silly thing, but it made such a strong impression, I can recall it as though it was yesterday. On the other hand, I'm not sure I could remember what I did yesterday.*

As the children grew older, they were given chores to help with the family ranch. The strong-willed Elizabeth insisted her two daughters, Josie and Ann, learn the same ranching skills. Ann later described the chores that went with a working ranch:

*We had to work. Horses, cattle, or sheep, as the case might be, required constant care. The farming, raising and "putting up" hay was a part time job. Our system of living depended on individual productive industry for its wellbeing. Staple groceries and clothing had to be hauled from Rock Springs, Wyoming, by wagons over rough roads, a hundred miles away. It required about ten days to complete the round trip. This was done spring and fall. There were only a few plows in the country. These plows, as were other farming equipment, were used or loaned all around the area where needed. Grain was threshed by driving horses over the bundles placed on the ground in clean swept corrals, and cleaned of chaff by a homemade fanning mill.*

When the chores were completed, the Bassett children often rode their horses among the hills near their home. Glade Ross, a lifelong resident of Browns Park, later related the following incident regarding Josie's childhood:

*Sam and Josie went up Bull Canyon to get horses. Sam on a scrawny iron grey and Josie on a sorrel mare which looked good but was not as good a horse as she looked. As they were coming back down, a tall man—ugly, dirty, red stubble about an inch long, riding an old grey horse just about played out—stopped them. He had corduroy pants on, stuffed in his boot tops, no sign of a gun and no pack or supplies. The horse was shod. Said, "Sis let's trade horses." Josie refused but he insisted, took her off her horse and changed saddles. Sam said, "Better let him do it, Josie," but Josie was mad and really cussed him out. He said, "O.K. kids, I'll see you around," and left on her horse. No one knows who he was, and Mr. Bassett tried to find out but never did. The grey horse was much better than the sorrel and Josie had him several years until he died. Everyone kidded Josie about being quite a horse trader, but she didn't like it.*

The education of his children was an important priority to Herb Bassett. He established the first public school district in northwest Colorado. Four students attended the first school term in 1881, held in the dugout home of Henry and Jennie Jaynes. The students included the two Jaynes children and the older Bassett children, Josie and Sam. Josie later recalled:

*In winter, of course, we had to go to school. I can remember when we only had three months [of] school. There was no district organized in having school; my father was trying hard to have a district. And there was only a few children. I went, but I wasn't old enough. I wasn't hardly school age, had to be seven years old then, and I wasn't. But I went and drew public money just the same, 'cause there had to be so many from a district to have a school district organized. Well, school was taught just over the rise towards the river, just directly between the river and the schoolhouse that is there now. We didn't have a schoolhouse; we had a barn: a big barn was built. And school was taught in the barn. My father partitioned it off with a tarpaulin, cut a window, and built a fireplace, and they had benches and a table and a teacher. Mrs. Jaynes was the teacher.*

Josie remembered the Christmas seasons with great affection. She later said:

*We had a Christmas tree. My mother was great on having a Christmas tree and homemade candy and popcorn and peanuts. And you know, they strung the berries from the wild rose bushes to decorate the tree. I strung many of them. [We] had a Christmas tree for all the children. You know, the old-time cowboys took an interest in that. That was a kind of curiosity to them. Some fellows, I can remember, came there and enjoyed that Christmas tree just as well as the children. Mother would bake pies and cookies and a lot of things. We had supper; sometimes they danced.*

In 1882 a stranger by the name of Hambleton, along with two friends, came to the Bassett ranch looking for one of their hired men, Jack Rolla. The strangers approached the corrals and, finding Rolla with his back to them, shot him in cold blood. Several ranch hands, along with Herb and Elizabeth, quickly ran to the scene, drawing their guns on the strangers. Ann's account of the horrible murder and aftermath, particularly regarding the actions of her parents, starkly contrasts Josie's account. Ann recounted:

*While Mother and Mrs. Jaynes were administering to the dying cowboy, Father and Perry were guarding the prisoners. Harry Hindle went to notify the settlers of the park, and to get Charles Allen, Justice of the Peace, to the scene of the crime. Night came and Father began to think with deepening apprehension. A lynching could be in the making. He advised the captives to go to the barn and feed their horses, and he warned them to ride directly to the county seat, over a hundred miles away, and surrender themselves to the law. When neighbors arrived at the Bassett ranch, the murderer and his companions had escaped. Naturally, they failed to do as Father had instructed, and were never heard of again. The method subscribed to my father in the matter of advice to the shooters would have been in direct conflict with the opinion of Mother and Mrs. Jaynes. Therefore, he did not commit himself and tell the true story for some time afterwards.*

Following the murder and the release of the "captives" held in the barn, Elizabeth was furious with Herb, according to Josie, and sent a few of her hired hands to track down the murderous outlaws. Josie later recounted her version of the events following the murder of Jack Rolla:

*However, the three men rode north instead, towards Rock Springs. My mother had gathered some of her boys, and when they arrived back at the bunkhouse to find the men gone, they set out immediately on their trail. Somewhere near the north end of Irish Canyon, they caught up to them. There was no gunfight, because the Texas boys had been disarmed at the ranch, and they were also outnumbered two or three to one. They were hanged and buried there in Irish Canyon. It was always said they left the country, but we all knew better. Jim [McKnight] told me all about it, and he should have known—he was there when it happened.*

Elizabeth continued her own personal war against the encroaching cattle barons. However, in 1889 Elizabeth's hired hands took things too far. (Subsequent court testimony would reveal no proof of Elizabeth's involvement.) Apparently, on November 5, 1889, Isom Dart, Jack Fitch, and Angus McDougall entered the home of Henry "Harry" Hoy and stole many items. The trio then torched the house, the barn, a shed, and the haystacks. Hoy swore out a complaint at the Routt County District Court in Hahns Peak. The charges against Dart, Fitch, and McDougall were grand larceny and arson. Hoy's brother, Adea, also filed a complaint against Dart and McDougall, charging them with altering the brands on three of his horses.

Court convened at Hahns Peak on January 21, 1890. The three accused men appeared before the judge to hear the charges. Bail was set at six hundred dollars for each man. Several Browns Park ranchers raised money for the bail, including J. C. Allen, C. W. Barrington, George Law, and Elizabeth Bassett. With bond posted, the three men walked out of court with the promise to appear for their September trial date. When court convened on September 9, 1890, Fitch and McDougall were in attendance. However, Dart did not appear, and it would be quite some time before he was seen again in Browns Park.

Prosecuting witnesses for the Hoys were William Ames, Perry Carmichael, Julia Hoy, Valentine S. Hoy, and John Martin. Among the witnesses for the defense were Elizabeth Bassett, her son Sam, and Thomas Davenport. Fitch was found guilty of arson and sentenced to five years in the Colorado State Penitentiary at Canon City. McDougall was also found guilty of arson and altering brands on the Hoy horses. He was sentenced to seven years of hard labor at the Colorado State Penitentiary.

For a time, the Bassett family continued with their daily routine. The Bassett sisters attended high school in the town of Craig, Colorado. The *Colorado Pantograph* of November 6, 1892, carried the following news tidbit concerning the Bassetts: "The Misses Bassett and Mr. Matt Rash arrived in the city Monday from Browns Park. The young ladies are here for the purpose of attending school, and are stopping at the home of Mr. Joe Carroll."

Josie later mistakenly recalled being fifteen years old when she met Butch Cassidy (alias George Cassidy at that time). However, the famous outlaw's presence in Browns Park was first noted in spring of 1886, when Josie was only twelve years old. Fond of horse racing, Cassidy rode a champion bay mare, owned by Charlie Crouse, to victory at a horse race

Butch Cassidy's mugshot (c. 1894), taken at the Wyoming State Penitentiary in Laramie

held at the nearby Beaver Creek racetrack. Josie and Ann had attended the race. Josie later said:

> *I thought he was the most dashing and handsome man I had ever seen. I was such a young thing, and giddy as most teenagers are, and I looked upon Butch as my knight in shining armor. But he was more interested in his horse than he was in me, and I remember being very put out by that. I went home after being snubbed by him and stamped my foot on the floor in frustration.*

Surrounded by mountains, with plenty of water and good grazing in the valley below, Browns Park seemed a perfect place for a hideout, and Cassidy took advantage. Forming his gang of outlaws, later known as the notorious Wild Bunch, Cassidy established his first hideout in the area around Browns Park. Among the various outlaws who visited, passed through, or made their home in Browns Park were Cassidy's close friends Matt Warner and Tom McCarty, as well as Elza Lay and Harry Longabaugh, the Sundance Kid.

Josie knew all these men. Of Warner, Josie later said, "Old Matt Warner that [Charles] Kelly writes about, why he was nothing. I'm not proud of the fact that I knew him." Regarding the outlaw element Josie commented, "The outlaw days of Browns Park were perfectly safe. I knew some people that were outlaws, of course, but at the time I didn't know that they were outlaws. They never left gates open."

Herb and Elizabeth welcomed the outlaws, provided shelter for them, offered them temporary work, and often did business with them, supplying them with beef and fresh horses. Josie evidently didn't mind the added company at all: "And let me say they had some cute boys with their outfit. It was a thrill to see Henry Rhudenbaugh [sic] tall, blond & handsome."

During that summer Cassidy spent a great deal of time around the Bassett ranch. He spent time with Herb, reading his newspapers and books. (Years later Josie would share a different recollection of twenty-year-old Cassidy, describing him as "a big dumb kid who liked to joke.") Cassidy often left the Park for months at a time. Even so, it was only a matter of time before Josie and Cassidy became lovers. Later Josie recounted this teenage affair of the heart:

> *After one of Butch's rich uncles died [euphemism for a bank or train robbery], we put him up, hiding him in the hay loft. He used to say, "Josie, I'm lonely up here. Come out and keep me company . . ." He asked me . . . "What am I going to do to keep from being bored?" Well, all I can say is, I didn't let him get bored.*

The affair ended when Cassidy left the Park. Josie later commented on this time and Cassidy in particular:

> *I knew Butch Cassidy a long, long time and so did my father before we ever believed that he was on the outlaw life. My father would never believe for a long time. He said, "That fella is not that kind of man." Hell, he broke horses for different people, worked with cattle and everything.*

Not long after Cassidy left Browns Park, Josie was sent to Craig to finish her high school education. In 1890, Herb and Elizabeth sent sixteen-year-old Josie to Catholic finishing school at St. Mary's of the Wasatch in Salt Lake City, Utah. Josie thoroughly enjoyed her time and education at St. Mary's. She fondly remembered her father's reading to her from the classics, such as Shakespeare, and she took this knowledge with her to St. Mary's. A very well-mannered and receptive student, unlike Ann, who would attend the same school a few years later, Josie received high marks in all subjects. However, Josie's schooling was sadly disrupted in December 1892, when her beloved mother suddenly died at the age of thirty-seven. Elizabeth woke early one morning when she heard a ruckus outside her window. Leaping from bed to investigate, she saw her favorite milk cow caught up in a herd of cattle being rounded up by the cattle barons. Furious, Elizabeth saddled her horse and rode out to claim her cow. With a few choice words, she cut her cow out of the herd and returned it to the Bassett ranch. It proved to be a trying day for Elizabeth, and she retired to bed early that night.

Mary Eliza Chamberlain Miller Bassett died the following day. She would be the first to be buried in the private cemetery on the Bassett ranch. Josie later recalled the event:

*She went to bed at night all right, and woke up about four o'clock in the morning just deathly sick. Just terribly sick. Father was there and Jim McKnight was there, and—I don't know—some of the cowboys. And they couldn't get a doctor, of course. All they could do—all they thought of was hot applications and that relieved her, of course, but she died.*

The *Craig Empire Courier* newspaper reported Elizabeth's death in its December 16, 1892 issue. The article misstates her age and the term of her illness:

### *A Sad Event*

*A messenger from Browns Park arrived Monday bringing the sad intelligence of the death of Mrs. E. Bassett. Her children, Sam, Josie and Anna who have been attending school, immediately started for home, accompanied by Mrs. William Morgan. Mrs. Bassett's death occurred on Sunday after an illness of two weeks. The deceased is one of the best known women in the county, where she has lived since the earliest settlement. She was a natural pioneer possessing the most remarkable courage and energy. She was highly esteemed by those who best knew her and commanded the respect of those who from conflicting business interests were her enemies. The most conspicuous and admirable trait in Mrs. Bassett's character was her unwavering loyalty and devotion to her friends. She was only 35 years of age and apparently in the meridian of health and vigor. The sympathy of the community is extended to the motherless children.*

According to writer Grace McClure, the only neighbor in the Park to "damn her" was Jesse S. Hoy. Having had several conflicts with Elizabeth and others, Hoy eventually stopped his attempt to overtake the small-scale ranchers in Browns Park. After her death, Hoy was quoted as saying, "We came into Browns Park to run the nesters out. We started it, but Elizabeth Bassett finished it, and she finished it good!" Perhaps. While it is not known which of the cattle baron companies attempted to steal Elizabeth's favorite milk cow, the act resulted in the early demise of the "natural pioneer possessing the most remarkable courage and energy," as the *Empire Courier* aptly characterized Elizabeth.

For Josie personal events surrounding the death of her mother would change her life forever.

# CHAPTER TWO

# Marriage and Murder

JOSIE WAS DEVASTATED BY THE DEATH OF HER MOTHER. SHE ALWAYS believed her mother died of appendicitis, while Ann believed their mother's death was due to miscarriage. The Bassett family grief was deep. The matriarch of the family and anchor, particularly for Josie and Ann, was gone. When Herb encouraged Josie to return to school at St. Mary's, she refused, telling her father she was needed at home. Josie later said, "I was away at St. Mary's when my mother died. I didn't go back, I stayed home then because my father needed me so bad. My father was perfectly lost. I had been two years at St. Mary's to November, two years and a half, pert' near."

This was a particularly difficult time in Josie's life, which accounts for her incomplete statement. Not only was she grieving the loss of her mother; she also came to the realization that she was pregnant with Jim McKnight's child. She hated to let her father down, but she had no choice. On March 21, 1893, Jim and nineteen-year-old Josie were married in Green River City, Utah. The couple returned to Browns Park, where Josie gave birth to a son, whom they named Crawford, on July 12, 1893.

Her father may have been disappointed but eventually welcomed the new family. On the other hand, Josie's uncle Sam Bassett offered her one of his mining claims, the surrounding land, and a cabin on the condition that she take care of him until his death. Josie agreed, and she and Jim, along with their baby boy, moved to Beaver Creek, at the edge of Browns Park. The couple built a cabin of their own near Sam's. Josie planted a garden, and Jim built a barn and additional buildings on the land. By Josie's own account, she enjoyed married life and got along well with Jim's family. She later recalled:

> *Jim's father had three wives, not all of them at the same time, but two of them at the same time. I knew both of them, and one of them died. His father was a very smart man, James Arthur McKnight. He once owned the* Deseret News. *He was an editor, a paperman [sic]. A very nice man too, I knew him very well. His mother was a Mormon, and she believed in it, she actually was an honorable person. And I respected her belief, although I would never listen to her. I would say, "Let's don't talk about it." He [James Arthur McKnight] left her and went to Washington and died there. He never married again but he had these two women. Jim's mother had seven children. That was cruel to leave that old lady with seven children.*

Although Beaver Creek ran through the McKnights' land, the high creek banks were above the level of their land. According to Bassett biographer Grace McClure, it was Josie who solved the problem of getting the water down to their land. She and Jim "cut an irrigation ditch extending four or five miles across the brush to a point where the creek came out of the hills, grading the ditch in a gentle slope to their land." The surrounding ranchers thought little of the effort, calling it "McKnight's Folly." Josie was confident in her idea, however, as it stood to reason "that the water would have to flow downhill." Josie was vindicated: she and Jim shouted with glee as the floodgate was opened and water gently flowed down through the ditch.

Josie loved ranch life. She enjoyed riding on horseback, checking the cattle, and observing the land. When she wasn't in the saddle, she cared for her family. This woman of diverse interests delighted in her domestic duties. While caring for her son, she also cooked, cleaned, and maintained the cabin for her family. She laundered their clothes in a washtub over an open fire in the yard, using homemade lye soap. She planted apple trees and harvested vegetables from the garden for the family meals. All the while, she managed to care for her ailing uncle.

In 1895 Ann returned from Mrs. Potter's School for Girls in Boston, Massachusetts. The following year she hosted a Thanksgiving dinner party for all the families in Browns Park. Held at the Davenport ranch, the event also drew Matt Rash, Isom Dart, Elza Lay, Butch Cassidy, and "Harry Roudenbaugh" (Longabaugh). Ann's memoirs describe the women's clothing in great detail. Of Josie's dress, Ann recalled:

*Josie's dress for the party was a sage green wool. Many-gored skirt, tight to the knees then flared to the floor to sweep up the dirt. Josie was married, I was not. By the way, Josie played a "Zither" and rather well. She was accompanied by Sam Bassett on the fiddle and Joe Davenport with a guitar.*

This account lends further insight to the character, talent, and diversity Josie possessed. A hard-working rancher, she could also grace social events with style and glamor. It is also a bit revealing as to the physique of the woman. When Josie wore the green dress "tight to the knees," she was pregnant with her second child. In the spring of 1897, the McKnights were blessed with a second son, whom they named Herbert after Josie's father but nicknamed Chick.

Following the death of Elizabeth, Isom Dart went to work with Jim. Although Dart had his own small cattle herd on Cold Spring Mountain, above the McKnight land, he had arranged a working partnership with Jim, much as he had had with Elizabeth. The relationship between Dart and the McKnights was a close one. Dart enjoyed spending time with the young McKnight boys and often stayed with them while the McKnights were away. He never tired of playing with the boys, and he would sing songs to them and play rodeo games with them, just as he had with Josie and her siblings many years earlier.

Josie often traveled by horse and buggy the ten miles to the Bassett ranch to visit with her father, brothers, and sister. Butch Cassidy had returned to the Park during this time, and Josie may have visited with him on these trips to the family ranch. One of the outlaws who had a cabin on Diamond Mountain was Matt Warner. It was his cabin that Cassidy and members of the Wild Bunch used as a hideout after their various robberies.

Josie detested Matt Warner and with good reason, given her personal experience with him and his wife, Rose. Warner would often leave his wife alone on Diamond Mountain while he was away committing a robbery. During one such occurrence it turned out that Warner had actually abandoned her. Mrs. Charlie Crouse enlisted Josie's help when it became apparent that Rose Warner was ill. Years later Josie spoke about the incident:

*Warner married a little woman, kind of a hillbilly girl, not bad looking. Her name was Rose Ramone and he took her over to Pot Creek, over the mountain to the Matt Warner place. It is still called the Warner Draw upon Pot Creek. I know where the old house was. He took her down to the ford in the river, you see there was no bridge over Green River then, you had to cross on the ice or ford it. You couldn't cross it when the water was high or ice was gully. So this little woman, she was a small woman, just a perfect little form, crossed the river. They lived with a man by the name of Bender [who] had a place there. He lived at the old Dr. Parsons place. Dr. Parsons is buried there. And Matt Warner and his wife camped there with the Benders. Couldn't live up there in the winter, it was too cold, they had nothing to live on anyhow. This little woman was sick. She had rode a side-saddle, where they had that big horn, you know what a side-saddle is, that horn that goes over your knee. It had made a terrible sore on her knee, it was awful, and she couldn't walk. And it developed into cancer, I learned afterwards. I didn't know then and neither did Mrs. Crouse. Mary Crouse came to me and said, "We got to go up and see what we can do for this Mrs. Matt Warner. She's up on at Bender's cabin and has a terrible sore on her knee, and she has no bandages. She has no towels, she has no nightgown, she has nothing." And the poor thing had a dirt floor and a big old fireplace. We took old shirttails and pillowcases, anything as bandages for the runny sore, an awful thing. Oh, it was great big, her knee was. I was never so sorry for anything in my life as I was for that pale, pitiful-looking thing. Mrs. Davenport didn't go up, because she was afraid of the river. Mrs. Crouse wasn't afraid, and I wasn't. I was afraid of that ice. We stayed there until the ice went away. The ice all floated down, and Mrs. Crouse took her to Vernal. I went with Mrs. Crouse that morning. Mrs. Crouse went over the mountain alone; that was a bad road too. It must have been March. She left there in the morning about eight o'clock. She had a good team and a good old salty mountain buggy, took poor old Rose Warner. Oh, it was terrible to have a woman off in that mess, awful, awful. Mrs. Crouse took her to her home in Vernal, and she stayed there and sent to Duchesne for the post doctor, and [the doctor] took her leg off between the knee and the hip. And after a while, about five or six months, she had a baby born. The baby was born at Duchesne. They took her down to the hospital at the post. And she died, and the baby was given to her mother or aunt, I forgot which. Anyway, some of her family took the baby; it was a girl baby. I never saw the baby, never saw her after Mrs. Crouse took her.*

Josie's dislike for Matt Warner only grew more intense after this incident. Josie later recalled:

*Matt Warner was nothing. He wasn't reliable, and he wasn't honest. He would rob sheep camps of beans, bacon, grain, whatever they had. Davenport knew that, everybody that had sheep. Crouse had sheep in the country then. Somebody, Mr. Saltmiller, he's a writer from over in Provo, I think, asked if I was afraid of him. I said, "No, I'm not afraid of him." He said, "He's a bad man." I said, "He's no bad man." I knew him for years and years, and the worse thing he ever done was rob a sheep camp. Nobody would hire him; he wouldn't work.*

Though Josie's recollections regarding Rose Warner are correct, there are a few gaps in the time frame. Rose Warner lingered between life and death at the Duchesne army post hospital for quite some time. It is also important to note that during this time Matt Warner was involved in serious crime, including bank robbery and murder. In due course, Warner was arrested, tried, and convicted in Vernal, Utah, for the murder of Dave Milton, Richard "Dick" Staunton, and Ike Staunton.

During Warner's time at the Utah State Prison, he received word that his wife had died of cancer. Warner was allowed to attend the funeral in Salt Lake City. Warner later recalled the episode: "I guess a man never went through more agony and lived than I did when they took me handcuffed between two guards to see my dead wife lying there in the coffin. That was all my past, all my responsibility rising up all together and handing me a knockout right on the chin."

In 1898 Josie suffered a devastating family loss. Her beloved uncle Sam died, having suffered a second stroke. Josie later recalled: "He [Sam Bassett] had a stroke and wasn't able; oh, he could talk, but he couldn't get around very good, and I took care of him as long as he lived, pert' near six years. Finally, he had another stroke, and that ended it."

February 1898 marked the beginning of the end for the outlaw element in Browns Park, spurred by two tragic events at the Bassett ranch. J. S. Hoy had filed complaints of cattle rustling and murder against John Jack "Judge" Bennett and Patrick Louis "P. L." Johnson.

Rumored to have killed a man, Johnson was leasing a portion of Hoy's land, and Hoy suspected he was the reason a few of his cattle were missing. Bennett had an interesting outlaw background. He possessed a long criminal record culminating with a charge of "assault with attempt to commit murder" following a December 28, 1887 incident in Lander, Wyoming. Convicted of the charge, he spent five years in the Wyoming State Prison in Laramie. Released on April 26, 1892, he roamed the Browns Park tri-state region, becoming a familiar figure. J. S. Hoy would later write, "Bennett was so handy with a gun that he thought no man or set of men dared to attempt to arrest him, and he had threaten[ed] to kill nearly every man in the valley. One man he had disliked in particular, and said he intended to 'shoot off an arm and a leg to see how he could move around.'"

Josie later said, "Johnson was a fool. He got in with Bennett, and Bennett used the Valentine Hoy place as a hangout."

In April 1897 Bennett was in Baggs, Wyoming, where he was involved in a kangaroo court of sorts at the Bull Dog Saloon. Participants included Butch Cassidy and other members of the Wild Bunch.

The Hoy complaint alleged that on February 17, 1898, at the ranch of Valentine Hoy near Pine Mountain along Red Creek, just over the state line in Wyoming, P. L. Johnson had shot and killed sixteen-year-old Willie Strang. An innocent action by the young boy had raised Johnson's ire: Strang had accidentally or playfully spilled water on Johnson's shirt. Johnson's reaction startled Strang, and he ran away from the scene. Johnson followed him to the barn, raised his pistol, and fired. The bullet hit the young boy in the back, and he died a few hours later.

Johnson and Bennett immediately left the ranch on a pair of Hoy horses, heading south for Powder Springs, northeast of Browns Park on the state line of Colorado and Wyoming. Forty-six-year-old Charlie Crouse formed a posse, which tracked the men as far as they could. Meanwhile, Valentine Hoy and William Pidgeon, a witness to the shooting of young Strang, buried the boy on Hoy land. Thirty-six-year-old Routt County Sheriff Charles Willis Neiman received the warrants a week later and on February 25 left the county seat of Hahns Peak with warrants in hand, though he knew Hoy's ranch was over the state line in Wyoming. (Jurisdiction in the Browns Park area was a difficult situation for the sheriff's department; this was the very reason outlaws chose the area as a hideout.)

Meanwhile, at Powder Springs Bennett and Johnson met up with two dangerous escaped convicts, David Lant, who had fled Utah State Penitentiary, and Harry Tracy, who had murdered three guards at Oregon State Penitentiary. The newly formed group hatched a plan. Bennett would stay behind to purchase supplies and would join the other three at Lodore Canyon, on the eastern edge of Browns Park.

Sheriff Neiman arrived in Craig, where he enlisted the assistance of Routt County Deputy Sheriff Ethan Allen Farnham. The men spent the night at the Vaughn ranch and left the following morning for the Bassett ranch, where they hoped to obtain information and raise a posse. Along the way they observed a group of riders. As Neiman attempted to approach them, the group fled. Arriving that evening at the Bassett ranch, the posse was greeted by sixty-three-year-old Herb Bassett; two of his sons, thirteen-year-old George and seventeen-year-old Elbert "Eb;" and twenty-year-old John Strang, the older brother of the murdered Willie Strang.

Following supper Sheriff Neiman persuaded Strang to ride out under the cover of darkness to recruit a posse. His intention was to ride off in the morning in pursuit of the men he had seen that day, as he had reason to believe Bennett and Johnson were among them. Shortly after midnight Strang returned with a group of men that included Valentine Hoy, William Pidgeon, E. B. "Longhorn" Thompson, Boyd Vaughn, and twenty-nine-year-old Jim McKnight.

The following morning, Monday, February 28, Eb Bassett and the other six men left the Bassett ranch with the sheriff and his deputy. They found the trail near where Sheriff Neiman had seen the men the previous day and followed it south nearly all day. At the base of Douglas Mountain, the men discovered an abandoned campsite with camp gear, bedding, and five horses. Obviously aware of being followed, the outlaws had left on foot for the rugged, rocky terrain of Douglas Mountain. The sheriff and his men knew it would be an ambush if they were to follow over the rocks with no trail. Therefore, Sheriff Neiman made the decision to wait them out. His theory was that the fugitives couldn't go far, because they had no horses, and with no bedding they would either come out of the rocky hills eventually or freeze to death in the cold February nights.

The next morning, March 1, 1898, the posse discovered fresh footprints in the snow leading to Lodore Canyon. The posse split up. Thompson and Strang stayed at the campsite with the posse's horses, while young Bassett and Vaughn were sent to a prominent rock point where they had a commanding view of the valley below and could stand watch in case the outlaws doubled back. Neiman, Farnham, Hoy, Pidgeon, and McKnight then set off on foot up the side of Douglas Mountain. About mid-afternoon Neiman knew his decision was the correct one, as the posse found a smoldering fire.

As Neiman was standing near the fire, Hoy started up the rocks toward a split rock. Neiman told Hoy not to get too far ahead of the posse just as Hoy stepped on a small rock. At that instant two rifle shots rang out in the rock canyon. Hoy fell, half sitting and half kneeling against the rocks. McKnight had been following Hoy up the rock cliff and now saw one of the outlaws, later recognized as Harry Tracy, jump out from behind a rock and attempt to grab Hoy's Winchester rifle. McKnight fired a shot toward the outlaw, who immediately ducked back for cover. For over an hour the posse hid in cover of rocks and cedar; the outlaws above clearly had the advantage. However, the outlaws' only viable escape route led through the rushing cold waters of the Green River. As evening approached, Neiman's posse, leaving Hoy's body behind, slid one at a time back down the mountain to the camp, where Thompson and Strang were holding the horses. With heavy hearts and no other options, the group of men left on horseback for the Bassett ranch, leading Hoy's horse.

On their solemn journey the group was met by Vaughn. He told the sheriff that he and Bassett had observed a lone rider who stopped and fired three shots in the air as he headed out of the mountain range. Waiting a few minutes, he fired again. Believing this was a signal to the outlaws, Vaughn and Bassett rode down to the valley and in a friendly, leisurely way, approached the man. Bassett recognized the man as John Jack "Judge" Bennett. Vaughn let the sheriff know of the scheme he and Bassett had quickly concocted: In a friendly gesture, Bassett invited the "stranger" to the Bassett ranch for the night. Accepting the invitation, Bennett left with Bassett; Vaughn explained he would soon follow.

Josie later talked about Eb's experience with Bennett:

> *Well, my brother Eb was just a big boy then, about seventeen, and he was scared to death of Bennett. Bennett was kind and pleasant to Eb, and Eb was to him, and they went home to Bassett's. My father had the post office, and he sold tobacco and little things like that. So Bennett said, "We're all out of tobacco," and that made Eb more scared than ever. He thought, "We! Who are 'we'? Wonder who the other people are."*

Meanwhile, Neiman and the rest of the posse rode hard to reach the Bassett ranch ahead of Bassett and Bennett. This was accomplished because Bennett's horse was obviously worn out, and he and Bassett rode at a slower pace. When Bassett and Bennett finally arrived at the ranch, Bassett corralled the horses while Bennett approached the ranch house.

Inside the Bassett home, Josie watched the arrival of her younger brother through the kitchen window. She and her two young sons had been staying at the ranch for safety after Jim joined the posse. Josie was baking a large batch of cookies when Bennett walked in. He checked his gun at the door, which was customary, and Josie invited him to have a seat at the table and offered him some of her warm cookies.

As Bennett was enjoying the cookies, Deputy Sheriff Farnham walked in. Farnham addressed the man, asking if his name was John Bennett. Bennett replied in the affirmative. Farnham then ordered the man onto his feet. As Bennett stood, Farnham showed him the arrest warrant for cattle theft and told him to put his hands up.

Over sixty years later, Josie recalled the incident:

*I had quit baking cookies to listen to what was going on. I was so scared. I could hardly speak, I was so scared. I thought, "Now, if he's got a six-shooter, he'll kill Farnham," but he had set his gun down at the back door when he came in. So he held his hands up high, and Farnham arrested him, put the handcuffs on him, and he didn't make much fuss about it. He swore and made a lot of threats about what he would do when he got loose. He was an impudent-looking man.*

Farnham took his prisoner to Herb Bassett's post office at Lodore, next to the Bassett ranch, which also served as a temporary jail when needed. Farnham handcuffed Bennett to a cot and guarded him. Bennett's verbal assaults against Farnham only increased.

In an interview years later, Josie said, "He carried on like a gray wolf. You never heard such terrible yells and screams and swearing. We could hear him from the kitchen, hearing him carrying on that way."

At noon the following day, March 2, 1898, seven masked men entered the temporary jail, leveled a shotgun at Farnham, and took his keys. They threw a gunny sack over Bennett's head, removed the handcuffs from the cot, and placed them on his wrists. While one of the men guarded Farnham, the others took Bennett out of the building and walked him toward the Bassett ranch. At the ranch the men removed Bennett's handcuffs, shackled his legs and arms, and led him to the ten-foot-high corral gatepost. Bennett was lifted onto a buckboard, and a noose was placed around his neck, the knot properly placed behind his right ear. The free end of the rope was then thrown over one of the pine gateposts. In a swift motion the masked men then drove the buckboard out from under Bennett. However, the drop was too short to break Bennett's neck, and he swung suspended for nearly four minutes before his body finally slumped in the cold mountain air.

Years later, Josie recalled, "I cooked dinner for the men who lynched Jack Bennett. At the time I didn't know what they'd done. After dinner I went outdoors to hang some dish towels on the clothesline, and there he was, swinging from the corral gate."

According to Browns Park historian John Rolfe Burroughs, Josie named three of the masked men as Harry Hindle, Lilton Lyons, and Jim Warren. When asked who the others were, Josie "pled forgetfulness with a twinkle in her eye."

Following dinner the men again donned their masks and returned to where Farnham was being held. They released him and rode away from the Bassett ranch. Farnham left the temporary prison and found Bennett hanging from the Bassett ranch gatepost. He cut down the body and dragged it up the draw above the ranch house. He then wrapped Bennett's body in a blanket, dug a shallow grave, and placed the body in the grave. After he covered the grave, Farnham placed rocks over it to deter coyotes.

Years later, Crawford McKnight, the older son of Josie and Jim, was interviewed by John Rolfe Burroughs. He said he and his younger brother didn't believe there really was a body in that spot above their grandfather's ranch. Crawford said he was about fourteen when he and younger brother, Chick, filled with curiosity, decided to find out for themselves if the legendary lynching story was true. They took a pick and shovel from their grandfather's ranch and walked up the draw behind the house to the grave site.

*Chick and I dug down two or three feet. I was swinging the pick and when it hit what seemed to be a hollow place, and when I raised the pick there was a skull on the point. Believe me, we scraped that skull back in the hole and covered it up in a hurry. We must have been a trifle pale around the gills when we went back to the house, because Granddad said, "Well boys, did you find anything?" We allowed as how we had, and were satisfied that the hanging really had taken place.*

The day after the lynching, Neiman split his posse into two parties. He sent each to watch one of the two exit points of Douglas Mountain in an effort to apprehend escaped convicts David Lant and Harry Tracy, now wanted for murder.

Meanwhile Sheriff Neiman, Eb Bassett, Tom Davenport, Pete Dillman, Longhorn Thompson, and Jerry Murray of the Utah posse left the Bassett ranch, heading toward the stage road near the Snake River. Neiman left his group, sending them to watch for the outlaws in case they crossed the river or waylaid the stage. Neiman and Bassett then backtracked to the Bassett ranch in an effort to hold the stage there. Dillman, Murray, and Thompson continued on. It was not long before they found a campsite where the fugitives had stayed. Near the campsite the posse discovered a gruesome scene. The partial remains of a horse were found; the outlaws had evidently cut out portions of horse flesh for consumption.

This Bassett buggy was used during the hanging of Judge Bennett at the Bassett ranch.

At a point a few miles south of Powder Springs, near one of the Davenport sheep ranches, Farnham, using field glasses, spotted the three fugitives sitting on a hill. Farnham and his posse rode toward them. As the outlaws saw the horsemen approaching, they slowly walked away. When the posse was within range, Farnham yelled to the fugitives to halt. The three men ran off in the opposite direction. The posse quickened its chase, and Farnham again ordered the men to stop. Johnson obeyed the order, turning toward the posse with his hands in the air. Lant and Tracy ran toward a hollow, where they disappeared.

In an interview published in the March 11, 1898 issue of *Rock Springs Rocket*, Davenport recalled the capture of the escaped convicts:

> *We then incautiously surrounded Tracy and Lant when they might have dropped all five of us. We did not realize what a desperado we had to deal with. They took refuge in a depression in the snow. I alighted from my horse, crawling among the greasewood until I saw Tracy's head sticking up. I didn't shoot. Lant, realizing that he was trapped, started to rise in order to surrender. But the dare-devil Tracy was gamey. He pointed his weapon at Lant and shouted, "Get down there, you blankety-blank blank." Lant then dropped back as Tracy shouted at us, "We'll tell you fellows we're quitting. But we want protection. We don't want to be strung up." After we guaranteed them safety, Lant appeared first with hands aloft. His feet broke through the snow as he approached, and he fell. Pete Swanson, thinking it was a ruse, shot Lant, but missed him. Tracy then reluctantly appeared, but with his gun in his belt. Knowing the man was desperate, Farnham took a quick shot at him on the spur of the moment, but also missed. It surprised the fearless outlaw, and he could not restrain his anger, but shouted, "You're a fine bunch of cowards, firing at a man with his hands in the air." We still didn't know we had such a noted criminal as Tracy until someone recognized him later. "Gents," he said, "give me a cup of coffee, a fresh horse, and twenty-five yards head start, and I won't bother you no more."*

Of course Farnham declined the request and handcuffed the men, and the posse set out for the Rock Springs–Browns Park road. In an ironic twist of fate, the posse encountered J. S. Hoy and Willis Rouf on horseback. Following the riders was twelve-year-old Felix Myers, who drove a buckboard containing a wooden coffin with the remains of Valentine Hoy. The group was riding to Rock Springs, from which point the body would be transported by train to the family home in Fremont, Nebraska. Though sympathetic to Hoy's situation, Farnham insisted that Hoy, as the police magistrate for Browns Park, return with the posse to oversee the trial of Johnson, Lant, and Tracy. Understandably Hoy was quite upset at the ironic turn of events.

Davenport later related the angry exchange:

*"Which one of you men killed my brother?" "Well one of us here did it," Tracy replied defiantly. We continued on down Irish and Bull Canyons to Bassett's ranch. As we approached the house, Farnham sent me ahead to tell the remainder of the posse waiting there that we had our men, and to keep cool and not get excited.*

The hearing was held in the large living room of the Bassett home, with Routt County Justice of the Peace for the Precinct of Lodore, J. S. Hoy presiding. The room was filled with witnesses and bystanders, including Herb and Eb Bassett and Jim and Josie McKnight. From the head of the Bassett family dining table, Hoy presided with remarkable composure over this legal matter related to the death of his brother. The accused, Lant and Tracy, mostly remained stoic throughout the proceedings, though Tracy displayed an air of contempt from time to time. After the hearing Hoy issued the following ruling, dated March 5, 1898:

*On the above date, P. L. Johnson, David Lant and Harry Tracy were brought before me by the Sheriff of Routt County charged with the killing of Valentine S. Hoy on the afternoon of March 1, 1898. I examined the three prisoners, the testimony of P. L. Johnson being in writing. The other two testified, but their testimony was not reduced to writing. I also examined Sheriff Charles Neiman, E. A. Farnham, and James McKnight. To me, the evidence taken and the circumstances surrounding the killing of Valentine S. Hoy was sufficient to*

*bind the prisoners over to the district court without bail, and they*
*were accordingly remanded to the custody of the Sheriff to be confined*
*in the county jail until the decision so rendered by due course of law,*
*except in the case of P. L. Johnson, who was turned over to the custody*
*of Deputy United States Marshal Charles Laney, who claimed John-*
*son on a writ of requisition from the Governor of Wyoming. Mitti-*
*mus remanding Lant and Tracy to the county jail contains the names*
*of the four principal witnesses in the prosecution, to wit: Charles*
*Neiman, E. A. Farnham, James McKnight, and J. S. Hoy.*

After Hoy's ruling reached the citizens of Browns Park, a large group
of men arrived at the Bassett ranch. According to Browns Park historian
John Rolfe Burroughs, "It was the largest congregation of law officers
and law-abiding citizens ever seen in those parts." With lynching in the
minds of many, Sheriff Neiman spent a long night discouraging the men
from such an action. At sunrise the following morning, the Wyoming
posse left the Bassett ranch with their prisoner, a shackled Johnson.
Neiman, cognizant of the lynch mob fever, left the ranch with Lant and
Tracy under heavy guard, traveling along backcountry cattle trails to
Hahns Peak and the Routt County jail. Shortly after arriving at the jail,
Lant and Tracy managed to escape, giving Neiman quite a beating in the
process. The two were apprehended twenty-four hours later by Neiman
at a stage stop near Steamboat Springs. Neiman then requested that the
Ninth District Court of Colorado, under Thomas A. Rucker, transfer the
prisoners to the more secure jail at Aspen, the seat of Pitkin County and
the court district.

Following these events, which essentially marked the end of the
outlaw element in Browns Park, residents returned their focus to the
ranching life. For Josie, that meant caring for her family back at Beaver
Creek. She enjoyed cooking and cleaning, doing laundry, and making
clothes for herself and her boys. She had planted a small orchard and
cared tenderly for the trees.

Although Josie and Jim were hardworking and ambitious, each had a
dominating personality, which caused friction in the marriage. Whereas
Josie was content, Jim was not. He began to spend more and more time

away from home. He frequented the Browns Park "Men's Club," a saloon operated by Charlie Crouse. Josie could not understand her husband's actions. She expected her husband to enjoy the warm family home she worked so hard to provide. Josie later said:

*I disagreed with him [Jim] because he was on the wrong track, I thought. I didn't like that whiskey business. I couldn't stand it. We never quarreled. We never had no home rows, no fussin', no quarrels atal [sic]. He always said I didn't have sense enough to raise a fuss. I raised one that lasted. Always left a fuss just where it landed. Wasn't no fuss atal, just an understanding. I said, "We live in two different worlds; you go your way, and I'll stay at home," and I did, I stayed. I had the ranch in Browns Park that is now known as the Lombard place, and that was mine. My uncle Sam homesteaded it and gave it to me. When I was married, he gave me the place with the under-standing that I was to take care of him as long as he lived; then he'd had a stroke. He gave me the deed to the place when he proved up on it, so that was mine, and that's what I told Jim McKnight. I said, "I'll stay home, this is mine; you go and do as you please. I think it's a foolish thing, but if that's what you want to do, do it."*

The troubled marriage escalated to a war of property rights. Jim wanted to sell the land, move to Vernal, Utah, and open a saloon. Josie refused. The couple fought constantly, and whispers of physical violence drifted through the community of Browns Park.

Finally, in March 1900, Herb Bassett took his daughter to Hahns Peak, the seat of Routt County, to file a restraining order against Jim. Divorce proceedings soon followed. Jim was furious. He not only rounded up their cattle and moved them off the land, he also took their children away from Beaver Creek and Josie. Of course, he had no legal right to do so, and Josie would find legal means to retaliate. In a taped interview, Crawford McKnight later recalled the unbelievable actions of his father:

*My dad kinda kidnapped me and my brother, took us to Salt Lake and then up to Smithfield and turned us over to old Aunt Jodie Heath. I don't know if she was dad's aunt really, but she was a fine old woman. I liked her a lot. Well, mother wanted us kids brought home, naturally, and she had papers made out, and they deputized a little guy in Rock Springs to come out to serve papers and a warrant for his [Jim's] arrest and a subpoena to appear in court.*

The April 14, 1900 issue of the *Empire Courier*, a Craig newspaper, ran a long article reporting more bloodshed in Browns Park. This time it involved Jim and Josie.

## *SHOOTING AT BROWN'S PARK*

*James McKnight Probably Fatally Wounded by Deputy Sheriff W. H. Harris*

*James McKnight, of Browns Park, was shot and probably fatally by Deputy Sheriff W. H. Harris, also of Browns Park, on Wednesday evening, April 4, about 9 o'clock at the Edwards ranch on Beaver Creek. Mrs. McKnight had obtained a summons and an order from the county court restraining McKnight from disposing of his property, and a bond for $2500 for his appearance, were placed in the hands of Sheriff Farnham to serve on McKnight at Browns Park. The Sheriff arrived at Bassett's on the 31st of March, a day in advance of Bassett and Mrs. McKnight. The Sheriff found that McKnight had already disposed of his property and left for Utah. . . . Not knowing whether or not McKnight would ever return, Sheriff Farnham appointed W. H. Harris, formally of Rock Springs, to serve the paper should McKnight return, and left for Craig.*

Local legend has it that Harris nailed the restraining notice on the Bassett gatepost, the very one from which John "Judge" Bennett had been hanged two years before. The *Empire Courier* continued its coverage:

*On April the 4th Mrs. McKnight sent word to her husband that she was very sick and wished to see him and "fix up matters." About dark he made his appearance. Those present at the ranch were: Miss Blanche*

*Tilton, Miss Ann Bassett, Carl Blair, Larry Curtain, Geo. Bassett, Eva Hoy, [Mrs.] Valentine Hoy, and Mrs. James McKnight. Mrs. McKnight was in bed and the women were giving her medicine and applying numerous mustard plasters. A little later, [Sheriff] Harris happened along and went into the house. [Jim] McKnight said, "How do you do, Harris?" and the latter replied, "How do you do, Jim?" Miss Tilton then invited both men to stay the night. Harris turned his horse in the corral and McKnight said he guessed he would go home, which is just across the line in Utah, and started for the door. Harris said, "Jim, I have a letter here for you to read" and handed him the summons which Jim read and threw on the table and remarked "that is only a matter of form." He then started for the door and Harris asked him if he could give bonds for those papers. He said "yes!" and started for the door again and Harris said he would put him under arrest until morning. McKnight did not answer, but opened the door and went out. Harris followed and called to him three times to stop but [McKnight] paid no attention to the command and Harris shot twice, one ball taking effect in the left side near the spine and glanced upward. Jim fell and called on Harris to shoot him in the head and finish the job. All rushed out of the house and the excitement was at a high pitch. Miss Ann Bassett, sister of Mrs. McKnight, being very demonstrative about the catastrophe which had befell her brother-in-law.*

Over time, local legend and some writers have propagated misconceptions surrounding the event, rather than relying on historical research. The most outrageous misconception is that Josie shot Jim. Though she wasn't present at the shooting, Josie responded to the accusation, "If I had shot him, I wouldn't have missed." Years later, Josie would further comment, "That's the main part of it, why the idea, the shooting. Why such a fool thing I never heard of. You know, I would like to refute that; yes, I would. 'Cause I have grandchildren and great grandchildren, I have an acre of them now."

Whether or not Josie was really sick is a matter of conjecture. However, what is known from Josie's own admission is that she sent her

Josie, second from left, with her two boys, pose for a picture during a visit in Craig following Sunday church services.
THE MUSEUM OF NORTHWEST COLORADO-CRAIG

estranged husband the letter to lure him into Colorado so that Deputy Sheriff Harris, who just so happened to be in the neighborhood, could serve him with the divorce papers.

The *Empire Courier* article ended with a strange twist of fate—one that would affect not only the McKnight and Bassett families, but all of Browns Park as well.

> *Hicks, [sic] new to the area, rode to Vernal, a distance of forty-five miles, in four hours and a half, and wired McKnight's relatives at Salt Lake and his [Jim's] brother, Frank McKnight, arrived Friday night and is looking after him. [Jim] McKnight signed the papers on the 7th and Harris came to Craig, arriving last Monday, and delivered them to Sheriff Farnham and returned to Browns Park on Tuesday.*

39

While a shooting in Browns Park obviously was newsworthy, the depth of the coverage regarding the McKnights' domestic situation speaks to the sensationalism of an era in which divorce was quite rare. This fact is reflected in the June 2, 1900 issue of the *Empire Courier*:

*There was quite a delegation of Browns Park citizens here this week. They left Thursday for Hahns Peak to attend the county court next Monday when the divorce case of Mrs. James McKnight against her husband will be tried before Judge Voice. Those who will appear in the case are A. H. Bassett, father of Mrs. McKnight, Miss Anna Bassett, George Bassett, Carl Blair, Joe Davenport and Mrs. E. B. Thompson.*

Another article in the same issue reported further details:

*Lew Ranney arrived here last Sunday from Browns Park. He accompanied James McKnight who was on his way to Hahns Peak to attend county court. Mr. McKnight has about fully recovered from the wound he received in April at the hands of Deputy Sheriff Harris. His injuries were not as serious as at first anticipated and, although three efforts were made with Xrays the bullet was not located and he still carries it as a reminder of his unpleasant experience.*

The June 16, 1900 issue of the *Empire Courier* reported the outcome of the legal proceedings:

*Mrs. Josie McKnight secured a divorce from James McKnight in the county court at Hahns Peak last week on the grounds of cruelty. Elaborate preparations had been made for a bitter legal fight on both sides, but Mr. and Mrs. McKnight, after meeting at Hahns Peak, decided between themselves to settle the question of allimony [sic] costs and custody of their two children out of court so as to avoid airing their troubles before the public. Mrs. McKnight left for Salt Lake last Tuesday for the children, armed with a letter from Jim to his sister, with whom they have been living, to turn them over to her. Mrs. McKnight will make her home in Craig with Mr. and Mrs. McLacklan for a short time. Mr. McKnight will embark in the sheep business in Utah. When they bade each other goodby [sic] at Craig no animosity existed between them and they parted with best wishes for each other.*

In their few subsequent meetings, Jim and Josie were cordial with each other, but their relations could hardly be described as friendly. As Josie later described her ex-husband, "He was undoubtedly Scotch. It was hardly in his favor. He wasn't a bad man—he was just a Scotchman, that's all."

Josie and her boys returned to the ranch on Beaver Creek, where she did her best to return to a normal life for herself and her children. Isom Dart came around from time to time to check on Josie and the boys.

However, that summer, murder rocked to their very core the lives of Josie; her sister, Ann; and all of Browns Park.

## Chapter Three

# Killer for Hire

WYOMING CATTLE BARON ORA HALEY HAD RECENTLY EXPANDED HIS ranching enterprise into Colorado. At Lay, approximately forty miles southeast of Browns Park, Haley set up the headquarters of the Colorado extension of his Two Bar Ranch cattle enterprise. Haley's registered brand was two slanted bars / / located on the animal's left hip.

Haley wasted no time in organizing other large cattle companies in Routt County to form the Snake River Stock Growers Association. The association's purpose was to gain control of Browns Park grazing land and drive out the small-scale, independent ranches, including the Bassetts'. The group included Haley's Two Bar operation, the Pierce-Reef Sevens ranch, Yampa Valley Livestock's Two Circle Bar ranch, and Charlie Ayer's Bar Ell Seven ranch. Also included in the group was John Coble of Wyoming's Swan Cattle operations. The association served as a "cattleman's committee" for its members, similar to the Wyoming Stock Growers Association based in Cheyenne.

The cattle barons considered anyone who contested their control of the open range a menace or, worse, a rustler. The committee soon grew to include five more Routt County ranchers. With such a large organization behind him, Haley moved his headquarters to his new ranch on the eastern edge of Browns Park, near the Snake River. Haley hired perhaps the best-known cattleman in the southern Wyoming basin, thirty-nine-year-old Hiram "Hi" Bernard, to run his newest cattle operation. Bernard had an impressive work history. He hailed from Texas, where he had worked with cattle on his family ranch. At the age of twelve, he herded cattle along the Chisholm Trail in an effort to help his family. After a few cattle drives north, Bernard settled in Wyoming, managing various cattle operations prior to being hired by Haley.

Local ranchers countered the threat of cattle barons' encroachment on Browns Park grazing land by establishing the Browns Park Cattle Association. Madison Matthew "Matt" Rash, Ann Bassett's fiancé, became the first president of the newly formed association. His first act was to establish a dividing line between Browns Park cattle and those of Haley's Two Bar Ranch. The line was drawn halfway between Snake River and Vermilion Creek, a north-south demarcation to which, for a while, the managers of the Two Bar Ranch agreed. Ann Bassett wrote of the new cattle association and Rash's leadership:

*Representing our cattle association, he [Rash] interviewed Hi Bernard in the matter of establishing a boundary line between Snake River and Browns Park. This resulted in an agreement between Bernard and Rash that the hills known as the "Divide," a range of limestone about halfway between Snake River and Vermilion Creek, extending north and south from the Escalante Hills to Douglas Mountain, was to be the western boundary for the Two Bar, and the eastern boundary for the Browns Park cattle. The arrangement was acceptable to all concerned.*

The boundary line was instrumental in forming a sizable opposition to the cattle barons and their attempt to encroach on Browns Park grazing lands and eventually take it over.

However, Haley changed his tactics. During a secret meeting held at Haley's office in Denver, the cattle barons each agreed to pay one hundred dollars a month to Charlie Ayer, who would then pay a private stock inspector to procure evidence of rustling in the Browns Park area. Bernard would later recount, "John Cobel [sic] offered a solution to the problem that would wipe out range menace permanently. He would contact a man from the Pinkerton Detective Agency. A man who could be relied on to do the job no questions asked."

In fact, the man Coble suggested the committee hire was none other than Tom Horn, a known killer for hire. Among the men who agreed to hiring Horn were Tim Kinney, the former owner of the Circle K Ranch, where Matt Rash once worked, and Haley. Hiring a mercenary killer would have seemed abhorrent to most folks, but apparently not to the tri-state area cattle barons.

In April 1900, a stranger had arrived in Browns Park giving his name as James Hicks and his occupation as ranch hand. He made his rounds in an unassuming manner, calling on various ranch owners including the Bassetts.

Josie later recalled the incident:

*I knew Tom Horn [alias Hicks] when he first came to the country. He came to the Bassetts' place. I lived at Willow Creek then. I was home when he came. He was a suspicious-looking man. He pretended that he was a horse buyer and wanted to stay there at the Bassetts. And my brother [Sam] said, "Why yes, you can stay here, we have horses to sell." He [Horn] wasn't a horse buyer atal [sic]. He was just looking around over the country to see who he was gonna get first. And after supper, I said to Sam, "I don't believe he's a horse buyer, I think he's a horse thief, something wrong about him. He don't look good to me." Well, he stayed there, and we all went up to look at the Bassett horses, eighteen miles up there. He was riding my brother's horse. He couldn't handle a rope better than I could. He was there for another purpose.*

Hi Bernard later recalled Horn's first rustling investigation in the Park and his part in it. Bernard said:

*Horn went to Browns Park. Soon after a bunch of twenty-eight head of well bred heifers branded V D belonging to a man in Baggs, Wyoming, were missing. Horn reported that he followed the small tracks of the cattle from the Snake River, east of Beaver Basin. Wiff Wilson and I went back with Horn and were shown parts of the trail. Wilson and I did not go all the way to Beaver Basin. Horn's statement had been verified so far, and we instructed him to make an effort to locate the cattle. Horn reported back to the committee that he had found butchered hides bearing the V D brand. One of the hides was found at Jim McKnight's summer cow camp at Summit Springs, and one at Mat [sic] Rash's N S Camp. Both places were at Beaver Basin. Horn brought the pieces of cowhide for Wilson, Ayers and me to examine. We wet and stretched the hides and found the V D brand on each piece. That looked like the boldest, most outrageous cattle rustling job I had ever seen or heard of. Acting for the general welfare of all range users adjacent to Browns Park, the appointed committee gave Horn the go ahead signal, and cautioned him to be sure he got the guilty men only.*

It is interesting to note that Bernard later commented on his involvement in the hiring of Horn. It had long been suspected that Bernard played a role but had not been proven. Bernard finally told the truth to his friend Francis "Frank" Willis during the summer of 1917. He had one condition: Willis was not to say anything until after Bernard was dead. Willis agreed. Willis recounted the incident in Bernard's own words in his working memoir, "Confidentially Told," which was never published. Bernard recalled:

*Haley sent for me to meet him in Denver. I met him there. Haley told me that Wiff Wilson and Charley [sic] Ayers were in Denver and had given him a tip on Browns Park conditions. Wilson and Ayers were prominent business and cattlemen of Baggs, Wyoming. They each had ranches on upper Snake River, and were old timers in the range country of Routt County.*

Interestingly enough, during that Denver meeting of the cattle barons, Bernard and Haley attended the second meeting where the men, led by Haley, agreed to the hiring of Horn. Years later, Bernard recalled the ominous occasion:

*Horn was not at the meeting and Coble acting for him said that Horn was to be paid five hundred dollars for every known cattle thief he killed. Haley was to put up one half of the money. Haley nodded consent to the agreement, but he did not commit himself in words. He instructed me to furnish Horn with accommodations and saddle horses at the Two Bar ranches. After the meeting was over, and Haley and I were by ourselves, he said to me: "Neither you nor I can afford to lay ourselves open to this man Horn. I do not want him on my payroll to kick back and collect money from me in a much more simple manner than by killing men for it."*

Bernard also recalled:

*A meeting was scheduled for nine o'clock that evening at Hayley's [sic] office. We went to dinner and returned to the office an hour or so later. Wiff Wilson, Charley [sic] Ayers and John Cobel [sic] came in. The business at hand got under way immediately with Wilson and Ayers bringing up the subject of range in Browns Park. They condemned the place as an outlaw hangout, and a threat to the Haley interests. Both men stated what they knew about the reputation of the Park, and Wilson from personal experience, giving detailed information regarding his losses, he attributed to the thieves of Browns Park and named Mat [sic] Rash and Jim McKnight as individuals whom he knew were cattle rustlers. I accepted their word at face value. If the [false] information, regarding Wilson's experience in Browns Park had been passed on to me at the time, as it was four years later, the entire affair might have been quite the reverse of what it was.*

Horn must have realized his ruse was not working with the Bassett family. It is questionable whether he knew of Ann Bassett's relation and engagement to Matt Rash. Nevertheless, Horn moved on to Rash's cabin, ostensibly looking for work. Rash hired Hicks as a ranch hand. The two were nearly inseparable as they rode together working on the ranch. On a typical day herding cattle near Cold Spring Mountain, the two happened upon Isom Dart, who was butchering a young bull. Both men saw rancher Sam Spicer's brand on the animal. Rash was shocked. He and Dart exchanged heated words as Horn watched.

On this occasion, Horn may have simply chanced upon the evidence of cattle rustling he had been charged with collecting. At other times, Horn fabricated evidence where it did not exist, according to Bernard.

Josie later commented on Bernard and his association with Horn. She said, "Hi Bernard was [the] Two Bar foreman, and the Two Bar was helping Tom Horn, furnishing him homes and horses to ride, when he was a cold blood murderer, cold blooded. Yes he was." Another area resident who met Horn, Allen "A. G." Wallihan, owner of the stage station at Lay, Colorado, commented on his impression of the man: "I didn't like him. He came here several times looking for some boots on the mail and when they did not arrive he got mad. My wife had lived all her life on the frontier, and she was not afraid of God, man, or devil, but she said: 'That man Hicks [Horn] is a bad man.'"

It is important to note that Wallihan's station was located in the vicinity of Haley's first Two Bar Ranch.

In early June 1900, dubious unsigned notices appeared on the cabin doors of the Park's more prominent cattle procurers, advising them to leave the Park within thirty days or else. The warnings were the subject of local gossip but were otherwise largely ignored. Matt Rash and Ann Bassett discussed the note they had each received. Concerned, Ann expressed her belief that it was a threat from Matt's former employee Hicks. Matt tried to calm Ann by laughing off the matter.

On the morning of July 7, Matt rode over to the Bassett ranch to see Ann. After a pleasant afternoon with his fiancé, Matt rode off to his cabin on Cold Spring Mountain. It would be the last time Ann ever saw Matt alive.

Three days later, on July 10, 1900, two teenagers, George Rife and Felix Myers, rode over to Cold Spring Mountain to visit with Matt. As they approached the cabin, an awful smell filled the air. Matt's favorite horse, which Elizabeth Bassett had given Matt as a gift more than ten years before, lay dead near the cabin. A dreadful fear overcame the boys as they cautiously approached the cabin. Inside, Myers found the dead body of Matt Rash. The stench was nearly overpowering, and flies were everywhere. Myers ran out of the cabin screaming for Rife. The latter determined that Matt, whose badly decomposed body had two bullet holes in it, had been dead for two or three days.

The boys rode off to find Deputy Sheriff Charley Sparks, who traveled to the scene of the murder and held an inquest. Following the inquest, Sparks and a few of his deputies dug a grave. The July heat had so decomposed Matt's body that the men covered their mouths and noses with cloths dipped in carbolic acid, so as not to breathe in the stench as they placed the body in the grave.

When Josie learned of the murder of her sister's fiancé, she immediately gathered her sons and headed for the Bassett family ranch. Josie did her best to console her younger sister. The *Craig Empire* reported the shocking news on their front page:

*Mr. Rash was lying on the bed partially turned over on his face, his head resting on his arm. Two bullet holes were found in his body, one through the back and abdomen, the other in the right breast. On the floor, between the bed and table was a pool of blood which had thoroughly dried. A chair was at the table and the condition of the dishes showed that Rash must have been eating a lunch at the time he was shot. While eating, he was facing a window in the west side of the cabin; behind him was the open door on the east side. Evidently Rash had been shot in the back and when he got up turned around only to be shot again through the right breast. He had fallen where the pool of dried blood was, then revived sufficiently to drag himself to bed. Rash had one boot off, which peculiarly is accounted for by the fact that he had always removed his boot as soon as he got into the cabin after he had been riding, the foot having been injured some years before and being sensitive, the rubbing of the stirrup caused him some annoyance.*

It is interesting to note that A. G. Wallihan, whose stage station lay some forty miles southeast of Browns Park, spotted the man known in the area as "Hicks" near sundown on July 8, 1900. Wallihan related, "I saw a man on a buckskin horse ride to the top of the ridge and stop and look back. Then he came right down to the crossing, and up the other side. He stopped when he got on top, and looked back again. I recognized him as 'Mr. Hicks.' A day or two after that, I heard that Matt Rash has been killed."

After Rash's murder, many of the Park's small-scale ranchers sought safety in numbers. Isom Dart was one of those men. With his sizable cattle herd, he joined in partnership with John Dempshire. The two shared a cabin belonging to Jim McKnight at Summit Spring on Cold Spring Mountain. The two men stayed at the cabin throughout the summer.

In early October a group of men stopped by to pay a visit. The group included Alec Seger; Griff Yarnell; and two of the Bassett boys, Sam and fourteen-year-old George. On the morning of October 3, 1900, the four men and young George left the cabin early, heading toward the corral. Suddenly two gunshots rang out in the solitude of the mountain morning. The shots hit Isom Dart, killing him instantly. The group frantically raced back to the safety of the cabin. They laid low inside the cabin until nightfall, when they slowly made their way out and down the mountain.

After the group reported their harrowing experience, several heavily armed citizens, including Josie, traveled on horseback to Cold Spring Mountain. The group found Dart's body approximately halfway between the cabin and the corral. A bullet hole in his body and another through his head, Dart was otherwise well preserved, due to the cool fall weather. As a few of the men began digging a grave, others in the party surveyed the area for any clues in the murder of their friend. A couple of the men discovered a spot at the back of the property where a horse had been tied to a tree for a long period. At the base of a large ponderosa pine near the edge of the corral, two .30-.30 bullet shells were found. The men were shocked at the discovery. Only one man in the area was known to carry a .30-.30 lever action rifle. That man was the stranger James Hicks—the same man who had helped Jim McKnight when he was shot the previous spring.

The group buried Dart just west of his cabin in a nice aspen grove. Afterward they solemnly descended the mountain, returning to the community with the news of their discovery. When the Routt County sheriff learned of the murder and evidence, the act was deemed the work of an assassin.

The Bassett children, and the second generation, Josie's boys, had known Dart their entire lives. Josie said of her longtime friend, "[He was]

Isom Dart, the Bassetts' beloved ranch hand, was murdered by Tom Horn.
DENVER PUBLIC LIBRARY, WESTERN HISTORY COLLECTION, X-21560

just a good, honest old colored man who never hurt anybody." The *Craig Courier* issue dated October 13, 1900, reported the murder:

*Another tragedy occurred in Browns Park Thursday morning of last week, Isom Dart, a negro, falling victim to an assassin's bullet. The murder occurred on the Cold Springs ranch. Dart and George Bassett were walking together from the cabin to the corral and when about twenty steps from the cabin door, a shot was fired from the direction of the corral and Isom fell dead. Young Bassett ran back to the cabin, in which were Sam Bassett and Lew Brown, who saw Dart fall when he was shot. The young men were afraid to venture out after the killing and remained in the cabin for four hours. Finally they left the cabin and started for the Matt Rash Ranch. The murderer had stood behind a tree 120 yards from where Dart fell. His tracks where he stood were quite plain and it was evident that the murderer had his horse tied a short distance behind him. The horse was shod and his trail was easy to follow. Sam Bassett and Billy Bragg followed the trail eight miles and when they quit it was perfectly plain.*

An inquest was held regarding the murder, at which time J. S. Hoy voiced concerns about the appointment of John Demsher as executor and manager of Dart's estate. At the time of his murder, the value of Dart's assets amounted to a little more than one thousand dollars, including personal property and thirty-six head of cattle. Demsher, who had a half-interest in the cattle, was selected by various citizens and friends of Dart, including Sam Bassett and Henry Hindle. Hoy's concern was that Demsher would move the cattle to Wyoming, which is exactly what he later did.

During the murder investigation it was discovered that just the week previous, on September 26, 1900, Horn, alias Hicks, had filed a complaint at the county courthouse at Hahns Peak, claiming that Dart had altered the brand on a horse belonging to Jim McKnight. Horn even named McKnight as a witness.

This claim was ludicrous on a few levels. First, at the time the supposed transgression occurred, McKnight was living in Utah. Second, if

Josie led a group from Browns Park up the mountain to bury Isom Dart on his ranch.
THE MUSEUM OF NORTHWEST COLORADO-CRAIG

McKnight had been present, why would he not put a stop to the supposed theft of his own horse? Even more incriminating was the fact that the claim was signed "Tom Horn." This was the first document linking the notorious Tom Horn to Browns Park. Nevertheless, authorities never followed up on the evidence, and the murder was never proven to be the work of Horn.

An explanation for the complaint's specifically naming McKnight can be offered. Horn had previously shown the recovered V D hides to the Snake River Stock Growers Association and had named his suspects: Matt Rash and Jim McKnight. Horn was given the "go ahead," as Hi Bernard put it, to proceed with the murderous task for which he had been hired, with one caveat: "to be sure he got the guilty men only." Following the murder of Isom Dart, who was not a suspect, Horn had to do some quick thinking. To cover for his mistake, Horn filed the erroneous complaint and in his haste mistakenly signed his real name. Bernard later made a chilling admission: "Horn made a further investigation and killed Mat [sic] Rash and Isam [sic] Dart, mistook by Horn, should have been Jim McKnight."

Following Dart's murder, the threats continued, and there was reason to believe that Josie's brothers were also targets of the assassin. The October 20, 1900 issue of the *Craig Courier* reported:

*A report from Browns Park states that a letter was found among the effects of Isam [sic] Dart, the Negro who was recently murdered there, warning the Bassett boys and Joe Davenport to leave the Park inside of 60 days or suffer the same fate which befell Matt Rash and Dart. The boys are interested in ranching and stock in Browns Park and were raised in that section. They have paid no attention to the warning and continue to attend their interests.*

This news arising so soon after Dart's murder, several heavily armed citizens, including Josie, took to riding the range divide that had been set up by Matt Rash. While Josie was riding the range, Ann stayed at the family ranch with their younger brothers. Ann later recounted an unnerving incident at the ranch shortly after the murders of Rash and Dart:

*Three months after the murder of Mat [sic] Rash and Isom Dart a man came creeping up to the house on the Bassett ranch. . . . I sat at a table in the living room playing solitaire. Four young boys, Carl Blair, Gail [sic] Downing and my brothers George and Eb Bassett, were lunching in the adjoining kitchen. Suddenly the night was shattered by blasts of gunfire. Two bullets came splintering through the door, embedding themselves in the opposite wall, less than six inches from where I had been seated. There could not be the slightest doubt for whom those bullets were intended. I dropped to the floor and rolled under the table. The boys doused the lamp and jumped to a side window, to shoot out into the night in the direction the gunfire had come. We remained in the darkened house and speculated on why our shepherd dog had not given the alarm of a night prowler's approach; he did not bark all during the night, which was most unusual. That faithful old watch dog never barked again, he had been strangled to death by the spiteful marauder. Fearful of being clipped by shots from ambush, we stayed in the house under cover until eleven o'clock the next day, when two ranchmen, Pete Lowe and Harry Hindle, drove up to the corral in a wagon.*

Hi Bernard did not think the notice or the shooting at the Bassett ranch was the work of Horn. Years later, Bernard told Frank Willis, "I do not believe that Tom Horn ever fired that shot. It is my opinion that someone from around Baggs got wise to Horn, they did the shooting and left a plain trail on purpose, so the Browns Park people could pick up a clew [sic] that would put them on Horn's trail. I have no idea who it was."

Several folks in the area left the Park, including E. B. "Longhorn" Thompson, whose ranch adjoined Haley's Two Bar ranch on the Snake River. Thompson moved his family to Vernal, Utah; Joe Davenport moved to Missouri. Shortly thereafter, Josie's brother Sam enlisted in the army, seeing action in the Philippines. Following his service, Sam relocated to Alaska and then moved to Washington. He never returned to Browns Park.

Even Josie, who loved her childhood home, felt it was time to leave.

CHAPTER FOUR

# Wanderlust

JOSIE HAD GROWN UP AROUND THE OUTLAW ELEMENT IN BROWNS PARK, yet she could never have imagined it would bring murder to her beloved homeland. Not long after the sad episode of Rose Warner's death, Josie began to think of leaving Browns Park for a new beginning. Josie found herself at a crossroad in her life. Her circumstances were different now: She was a single mother in a man's world. Somehow she needed to make a living for herself and her sons. Reeling with emotion following the deaths of Matt Rash and Isom Dart, her divorce, and her longtime friends' leaving Browns Park, Josie felt vulnerable for the first time in her life. She turned to her father for advice. Although Josie would take his advice, she always regretted her decision, as is clear in the following excerpt from her taped interview:

> *My father thought that the . . . [pause] He said—that was wrong of my father—he said, "Now a woman with two little children to send to school has no business living alone on the ranch." I had six hundred and eighty cattle, and I could have managed that outfit just as well, far better than I could living in town, because I wasn't used to that town business, and I don't like it and never did. George Bassett could have helped me and would, and that's why I should have stayed. But I sold out on father's advice and went to Craig and went into the hotel business, something I didn't know a thing about. But I made out all right. I made a living and lived very decent.*

Josie and the boys moved to Craig, where she leased the Elmo Hotel on the main street of town. As was typical of hotels at the turn of the century, the first floor contained offices, a dining room, and the kitchen. Rooms for the guests and boarders were on the second floor, as were separate living quarters for Josie, Crawford, and Chick.

Josie enrolled the boys in school and renewed old friendships with many folks she had known in Craig over the years, including Charles A. Ranney, who had been the high school principal when she attended school. A member of one of Craig's leading families (Ranney Street having been named for the family), Ranney was grand master of the Masonic lodge and owned the town drugstore.

Ranney became interested in Josie, and the two began to court when Josie could find the time away from her hotel. He took her on long buggy rides, and the two fished in the rivers, an activity Josie truly enjoyed. When Ranney proposed marriage, Josie, a divorced woman in an era when divorce was frowned upon, readily agreed. After all, a respectable man of means would support her and the boys, and she could finally get out of the hotel business she so detested.

In late January 1901 Josie rode over to Browns Park for a visit with her family. While there she came down with a severe case of mumps. The *Craig Courier* carried the story in its February 16, 1901 issue:

> *Josie McKnight returned from Browns Park Thursday. Upon her arrival in the park she was exposed to the mumps and remained there longer than she intended in order to be sure that she would not contract the disease and carry it to Craig. After staying in the park fifteen days and there being no indication of the disease attacking her she concluded it safe to return to Craig. However, Mrs. McKnight did not reckon correctly with the style of mumps she encountered and she now has a well developed case of the malady. She is stopping with Mrs. E. B. Thompson and that lady is enforcing a rigid quarantine at her home.*

In April 1902 twenty-six-year-old Josie Bassett McKnight married thirty-three-year-old Charles Ranney. The April 26, 1902 issue of the *Craig Courier* reported the event:

*C. A. Ranney and Mrs. Josie McKnight were united in marriage Thursday afternoon by Rev. H. E. Anderson. The wedding occurred at the Tucker residence which Mr. Ranney recently purchased and refitted in anticipation of this happy event. The marriage was strictly a home affair, only relatives of the young people being in attendance.*

Josie rid herself of the hotel, moved into the splendid home with her sons, and settled into what she anticipated to be a life of bliss. It was not to be. Almost from the beginning there was domestic tension inside the Ranney residence.

As Josie was dealing with her domestic issues, her sister Ann shocked the family and the entire Browns Park community when on April 13, 1904, she married Hi Bernard, the foreman of Ora Haley's Two Bar Ranch. Josie questioned Ann's judgment. She would later say, "When Ann married Hi Bernard, we all objected to that. I never said so to her because she was twenty-three years old and old enough to know what she was doing. She absolutely didn't. Hi Bernard wasn't on the right tracks. He had helped Tom Horn."

Just the previous year, Tom Horn had been tried and convicted for the murder of fifteen-year-old Willie Nickell, in Laramie County, Wyoming. On November 20, 1903, Horn was hanged in the heart of downtown Cheyenne, Wyoming.

With the murder conviction and subsequent hanging of Tom Horn, alias James Hicks, the stranger who had immediately aroused suspicion in Josie and Ann, Josie's long-held belief as to the man's character was confirmed. To Ann, justice had been served for the cold-blooded murder, even if it wasn't justice for her fiancé Matt Rash and longtime family ranch hand Isom Dart. Reflecting many years later on this notion of justice, Hi Bernard would say:

*Horn was not the only one connected with that affair [murder] that should have been hanged. There were several of us that the country could have gotten along without. It always puzzled me why Wiff Wilson and Charley Ayers [sic] were over anxious to move in on Browns Park for the kill. Their ranches and range was about one*

The Ranney family was very prominent in Craig. Standing in the middle is Charles A. Ranney, Josie's second husband.

*hundred miles from the Park, and they never ranged any stock near the place.*

Meanwhile tension mounted in Josie's new home in Craig. Her sons Crawford and Chick hated their new stepfather. Ranney, a strict disciplinarian, took a hard stance with the boys from the beginning. Crawford, who had his grandfather Bassett's mild, gentle nature, never understood Ranney's cruel actions. Chick, on the other hand, though engaging and outgoing, possessed the same strong-minded will and ambition as his grandmother Elizabeth Bassett and aunt Ann Bassett Bernard. Chick was constantly scolded, whipped, and demoralized by his stepfather.

Finally Chick had had enough. At the age of eight, the strong-willed kid saddled a horse and left for Browns Park. As the sun went down and the coyotes began to howl, however, Chick returned home. The event was not lost on Josie.

Evidently Josie had accepted the marriage of her sister to Hi Bernard, known to have aided and abetted the killer for hire Tom Horn. She wrote to Ann, who had recently moved to Douglas Mountain, asking if she would take in her youngest son.

Ann and Hi agreed. From then on Chick lived in Browns Park with Aunt Ann and Uncle Hi and stayed with his mother in Craig during the school term. Ann and Hi both grew very fond of the boy. They understood his wild nature and were patient with him. Hi had his own manner of discipline tempered with individual attention and understanding. Hi treated Chick as a man and expected the same in return. Hi introduced ten-year-old Chick to the cattle experience, and Chick was a quick learner. Hi took him to a spot on the Green River where cows often got stuck in the slimy mud. He helped Chick pull the animals free and let him rescue the calves of cows that could not be saved. He then gave the dogies to Chick to raise and care for. A mutual regard formed between the two, and for the first time young Chick respected authority. The Bernards bought Chick clothes, boots, and a saddle. Hi and Chick would often ride horses over to Craig or even north into Rock Springs, Wyoming. The two grew very close—so much so that when Hi drew up his will after his divorce from Ann, he left everything to Chick.

Remaining meanwhile with his mother and stepfather, mild-mannered Crawford would later comment on living with Charles A. Ranney:

*He was not malicious but he was hell on discipline. He was a school teacher and we kids had to stay in line. Like the Army, you ask? Hell, it was worse than the Army. In the Army there's a certain slack but there wasn't any slack around him! If he said "Bounce!" You better bounce. He's been a strict old bachelor too long. I minded my mother because she made me want to mind her, but he was cold to everybody, with not a very definite sense of humor.*

The opening of a new drugstore in Craig soon placed competitive pressure on Ranney, and his disposition at home worsened. He eventually sold his drugstore and bought a ranch on Fortification Creek. As pleased as Josie must have been to return to ranching, domestic life did not improve. The couple began fighting and hurling verbal assaults at each other.

Josie had finally had enough. After nearly four years of marriage, Josie packed her bags, and she and Crawford left the Charles Ranney home for the last time. They relocated to Baggs, Wyoming, where Josie opened a hotel, The Ranney House. She ran advertisements in several newspapers: An ad in the November 16, 1905 issue of the *Routt County Courier* boasted "New Beds" and "Perfectly Clean." In July 1906 Josie secured a divorce from her second husband. Josie would always remain vague about this period in her life. Being raised as a Catholic and going through two divorces must have weighed heavily upon her. However, she would later state in a taped interview,

"I would have stayed with Mr. Ranney—he was a fine man—if he hadn't been so hard on the children."

Evidently there were no hard feelings once the divorce was final. Josie and Charles Ranney corresponded over the years, as is evidenced by a letter Ranney wrote to Josie during the Christmas holiday of 1915:

*My dear old sweetheart; Being particularly sociable tonight (as I am all alone) I'll write you a few lines in answer to the great kick you put*

*up. None of us knew you where you lived: Lymon said "in a canyon away over in those mountains along Green River." I believe everyone in the party would have been pleased to have seen you. I looked every day for you as it was big doings in Vernal. I worked my best to gauge the trip so we would spend the 4th in Vernal. Wonder why? Maybe you were not very much put out for it took from July to December to work up that grouch. Now let's be good for you are the only wife I ever had and I don't want to quarrel and I don't believe you do. I expect always to think lots of you. . . . Give Dad [Herb Bassett] my kindest regards. I believe he is my friend. I got a dandy vote from Browns Park and I credit much of it to him. Give my best to your boys. I would like to see them. Tell them to come and see me if they ever get up this way. And now, wishing you a merry Xmas and everything good for the future. I remain the same old scout only a little older. My hearty good will and best wishes be with you. Chas to Josie.*

It is quite possible that Josie found another reason to leave Ranney: another man. For on July 12, 1906, as soon as her divorce was final, she married Charles Williams, another druggist, in Baggs, Wyoming. Crawford later described his second stepfather as "a railroad man and a prizefighter who was also a pharmacist." He called Williams a good man, a "city man who didn't like the country." Crawford said they later lived in Browns Park. Josie's sister Ann told her dear friend Esther Campbell that Williams was a "sports promoter." An issue of the *Craig Courier* dated October 16, 1905, ran the following notice: "Charles Williams, Snake River's favorite 'pug' will go to Craig and Hayden to fight a match with someone who has been sending challenges from that country."

In November 1906, after just four months of marriage, Josie Bassett McKnight Ranney Williams filed for divorce. She listed the cause as "desertion." She then threw caution to the wind and, in spite of her Catholic upbringing, married Emerson "Nig" Wells six months later. The two moved back to Browns Park.

Esther Campbell was a dear friend to Josie and Ann Bassett.

Years later and well into her eighties, with decades of emotional reflection, Josie commented on this period of her life:

*I wanted to do something, to get away off somewhere. I wanted to be in the hills—I don't know what I wanted. I didn't want to be in town. I knew I had to [be in town] at school time. And every year as long as the boys went to school I went with them. I went and located right there so I knew where they were every night. They finished school in Craig, and then they finished high school in Baggs. And then they were ready to go to Rawlins, the both of them. Then Crawford went to Mary University in Rock Springs and Chick "outlawed" on me and went home, back to Browns Park, and went to work with cattle. He wouldn't go to the university, said, "I'm not interested and I'm not going to stay." Then he went home to my father. Then Crawford finished in the university and both went back to Browns Park.*

When newlyweds Josie and Emerson Wells returned to Browns Park in 1911, they rented the old Davenport ranch, now owned by the bank. Wells, once a range foreman, began his own cattle ranch. Josie was happy to be back in her homeland and once again ranching, her true love. Wells was a likable fellow. Crawford said he was "a helluva nice guy." Yet Wells was also an alcoholic. As time went on, his health began to suffer. Josie insisted he see a doctor, who confirmed the drinking as a contributing factor to Wells's health condition.

Wells refused to stop drinking. He would often come home in a drunken, delirious stupor. Raised by her temperate father, Josie did not like liquor, yet tolerated her husband's drinking until it got out of hand and affected his health. Josie decided to take matters into her own hands. She saw an advertisement for the Keeley Cure, touted as "a positive and permanent cure for liquor and drug addictions." Josie purchased the product, a concoction of caffeine and tartar emetic (a heart depressant), which produced vomiting when ingested. Josie put the concoction in her husband's coffee, but it did not stop Wells from drinking.

In 1912 Josie and Wells made plans to attend the Christmas holidays at Linwood, located on the Utah-Wyoming border. The couple left early for Linwood because a snowstorm had been forecasted. Josie would later recall the trip: "We arrived at Linwood after driving from Browns Park in a buckboard in one of the coldest blizzards of the year. We didn't plan on staying as long as we did, but the snow was so deep and the wind blowing so cold."

In light of her husband's condition and the prospect of much festive drinking, Josie had been reluctant to even make the trip, yet she and Wells had followed through with their plans. Now the snowstorm continued, and the couple was forced to stay at Minnie Crouse Ronholdt's boardinghouse. This presented an uncomfortable situation for Josie, as she and Minnie, the daughter of Charlie Crouse, had never gotten along while growing up in Browns Park. Unfortunately, the circumstances would evolve from uncomfortable to tragic, as reflected in Josie's subsequent recounting of New Year's Eve 1912:

*He [Wells] was a good man, a good farmer and as good a man as ever lived, and he got on those whiskey drunks and went like foolish people. I didn't want to go, but the Rifes came—Guy Rife and his new wife and another Rife boy and his wife—and they wanted to go to Linwood. I didn't want to go. I thought, now if we go there they'll all get drunk. Wyoming was a regular honky-tonk and those men proceeded to go to that honky-tonk and get drunk. Well there was a dance and I stayed at the hotel with Mrs. Rife—we had rooms at the hotel [Minnie Crouse Ronholdt's boardinghouse]. Mrs. Rife's husband, Orin Rife, he didn't drink at all, but he couldn't get those fellows to the room to save him. Mrs. Guy Rife wanted me to go with her to the saloon to get the men. I said, "I didn't take them there and I never went to a saloon ever, and I'm not going." I knew an old Mexican. He worked in Browns Park—forget his name, old Joe something, an old man. He came over and told me, "I hate to tell you, but Wells is terribly drunk. They're running a game and I stole his watch away from him and I brought it to you." Well, I didn't know what to do. I couldn't get him away from there. We danced the first night. I went to the dance and tried to stand it all I could. I couldn't do anything else. I went with Minnie and a whole crowd of women and went to the dance. That was New Year's Eve and they danced all night till sunup. I didn't. I went home and went to bed. The next night they danced again. I went for a little while, and went back and went to bed. The next morning there was a man from Kansas City—a horse buyer, I forget his name. He was a very nice man, and he came to me and said, "I think your husband is ready to quit drinking." He said, "He's down in the living room." I went and he was there. I said, "Wells, I brought you a cup of coffee. Do you think you can drink it?" He said, "I'll try. I feel like hell this morning." I said, "As soon as it comes sunup time, we'll start for home." We had a team that wasn't very safe, kind of a tricky outfit. But I thought, I can drive anything to get out of here. So he drank a little of the coffee and he didn't drink any more. I helped him get his shoes on and helped him get his sweater on. Then I got a basin of warm water for him to wash his face and I said, "Now, if you can eat some breakfast, I'll bring it over here. I think you're too shaky to go up that hillside with ice on it, back to the other hotel." He said, "I won't want any breakfast, I feel like hell." He kept saying that to me and I said, "I'm awfully sorry, but I can't help. You did it yourself." He kept acting like he was sick to his stomach, and I said, "Are you going to throw that whiskey up? I wish you would." So I got a slop bucket and set it there by him—and I saw that something was wrong. The horse buyer said to me, "If I was in your place I'd give him a drink of whiskey. He needs it." And I said, "I think he needs anything but a drink of whiskey, but if you think that's all right, I will get it." I gave Wells a drink, then combed his hair and put the bottle back. Well, he kept turning, kind of twisting around like he was in misery somehow, I don't know what. But I knew he was wrong. And finally he just straightened right back and died. He threw up a little kind of foam, right from his lungs of course. Well, I laid him down and I didn't know what to do. I was stranded. I was just—I might as well have been drunk. There I was, clear up in Linwood thirty miles from home.*

Charley Olmey, a cowboy from Browns Park, also attended the New Year's celebration in Linwood. He offered to take Josie's buckboard and horses to the nearby town of Green River, Wyoming, to buy a casket.

Meanwhile, several women prepared the body of Emerson Wells and laid it outside the hotel in the freezing January air. The local authorities visited Josie and examined the body and the room where the death occurred. However, there was no one in the small town to perform an autopsy or sign a death certificate. When Olmey returned the following day with a pine coffin, Josie was allowed to take the body of her husband back to Browns Park. Josie would later relate the solemn event:

*We put the body in a homemade pine box put together by M. N. Larsen, and loaded it in the back of the wagon, and drove back to Browns Park in freezing weather. We took him back there, and then the next day I took him down and buried him by Uncle Sam, down in that cemetery. It was on the—he died on the third day of the month of January and was buried on the seventh. And the whole country was there. There were lots of people in Browns Park there, lots of people.*

Suspicion and rumors were whispered almost from the moment Wells's body was laid in the casket. How was it possible that a relatively young man could die so suddenly and for no reason except a three-day drunk? The rumors were fueled by none other than Minnie Crouse Ronholdt. Perhaps out of spite from childhood days, Ronholdt spread gossip that Josie had poisoned her husband. She claimed she had overheard the couple fighting and had personally witnessed Josie's preventing a woman from taking a glass of milk to Wells. There were many who did not believe Ronholdt's wild accusations against Josie, pointing to the fact that Josie had been questioned and cleared by the Linwood authorities.

One such person was Ford DeJournette, who had a ranch at Diamond Mountain in Browns Park and had been present at the New Year's Eve festivities. DeJournette's son, Richard "Dick," later shared the following account, as told to him by his father:

*On January 1, 1913, a big dance was held at Linwood. Ford DeJournette wasn't much of a dancer, but he liked to play cards. He was with Bill Garrett, the man who broke horses for him, and a horse buyer at Minnie Crouse Ronholdt's boarding house. The men were playing poker. Josie Bassett Wells and her husband, Nig [Emerson] Wells were at the dance. They were there for two or three days. Nig Wells got to hitting the jug and got extremely sick. Josie could never tolerate the drinking of alcoholic beverages. The men were downstairs playing cards and drinking. Nig Wells was upstairs in a room, and the card players could hear him hollering as if he were in a lot of pain. It wasn't long before Josie came down the stairs and told the men that Wells had died. Ford never had much to say about it one way or another. He just mentioned that Nig Wells did a lot of hollering. Minnie Crouse always accused Josie of poisoning him, but it was probably the rot-gut that did it.*

Undaunted, and evidently on a personal quest against Josie, Ronholdt took her accusation further, so sure was she of Josie's guilt. She wrote an article for the *Green River Star* newspaper in which she hinted at the poisoning theory: "It is the opinion of those who saw Wells just before he died that he swallowed poison, perhaps strychnine, as his actions were similar to the actions of men who had been known to die of the effects of an overdose of that drug."

However, the newspaper refused to publish the accusatory article. Ronholdt nevertheless spread the rumor, and several people not only believed her but perpetuated the myth. As the rumors spread, other stories filtered throughout the Park, growing to ridiculous dimensions. It was said that Wells's grave had been dug up and there was no body in the coffin. Once again, this rumor was started by Minnie Crouse Ronholdt:

*The only law around was Justice of the Peace Ed Tolton, a middle-aged man. Josie told him that Nig had fits and seizures and just wrapped Ed around her finger. Everything was in her favor, so she brought Nig back to Browns Park and said she buried him in the Lodore Cemetery. But many said the casket was empty, and so, no one knows where he's buried.*

Some even said the sheriff of Vernal, Utah, had dug up the grave. No matter that the gravesite was located in Colorado, where he would have been out of his jurisdiction. Nevertheless, this story was told and retold alongside wild speculation that Josie must have dumped Wells's body somewhere along the road between Linwood, Utah, and Browns Park, Colorado. Dick DeJournette may have wondered about the rumors concerning Wells's burial, as he wrote: "Josie buried Wells in Browns Park. It has been said, 'The body didn't stay put in the ground very long.' I don't know if anyone today knows just where he did finally find his resting spot."

Obviously, none of the rumors were true. Despite a few authors' writings to the contrary, the authorities never suspected Josie of any wrongdoing regarding the death of Emerson Wells. Even so, Minnie Crouse Ronholdt, who later married George Rasmussen, never let go of her belief that Josie had poisoned her fourth husband. In interviews held many years later at the Uintah County Library in Vernal, Utah, Rasmussen retold her accusations against Josie. Well into her nineties, she harbored accusations that had grown to include the theft of personal items such as embroidery and baby dresses. Years later, Josie's son Crawford commented on the actions of Minnie Crouse Ronholdt Rasmussen: "She [Rasmussen] was a hateful, spiteful little piece of furniture. If she didn't like somebody she'd pour it on 'em. I never did see eye to eye with Minnie." Josie had no patience for the gossip and rumors, and they must have affected her as she grieved the loss of her husband and found herself alone. The thirty-nine-year-old widow began planning her future. She did not have enough money to buy the Davenport ranch where she and Wells had lived. While looking into homesteading a place of her own, Josie continued to operate the ranch with Ben Morris, the ranch hand previously hired by Wells.

Because Wells had hired Morris, a thirty-four-year-old Oklahoma cowboy, Josie trusted him. He was good-looking, had a great sense of humor, and was dependable around the ranch. It wasn't long before the working relationship between the two became intimate. Yet Morris was not at all as trustworthy as Josie thought. In the summer of 1913, Josie's oldest son, Crawford, rode over from Craig for a visit with his mother. During his visit he observed a couple dozen corralled sheep with a nose brand belonging to Henry Nebb, for whom Crawford had once worked.

Years later, Crawford would remark on the character of Nebb: "He was a nice fellow and an honest one. If he owed you a nickel you'd get it."

Crawford confronted his mother about the sheep. When Josie said she knew nothing about them, he told her they were stolen sheep. Again Josie denied any involvement. In a disgusted rage Crawford stormed out of the house and rode directly to the home of Henry Nebb. He told Nebb he had found Nebb's sheep at his mother's ranch. Nebb said he had suspected his missing animals were at Josie's ranch. Not wanting to cause trouble with Crawford's mother, whom he believed innocent, Nebb told Crawford that something needed to be done. Crawford offered to drive the sheep to Nebb's ranch, and then he did so.

Crawford and his younger brother Chick confronted Morris about the stolen sheep. A surly and abusive Morris countered, telling the boys it was none of their business. A fight ensued. Morris was a large man, and when he swung at one of the boys, the other reacted. It took both boys to subdue Morris. Chick hit Morris with the butt of his gun. Morris fell to the ground, unconscious. Josie looked on, helpless to stop the fight. When it was over she had a few words for her sons, and they had a few words for her regarding the thief with whom she had taken up.

This incident separated mother and sons for several years. Crawford and Chick would later join their father Jim McKnight in his ranching enterprise in Utah.

For whatever reason, despite alienating her sons, Josie stood by Ben Morris. At least for the time being.

# CHAPTER FIVE

# Cub Creek

JOSIE HAD BEEN LOOKING FOR A PIECE OF LAND WHERE SHE COULD FILE a homestead. She finally found it approximately fifteen miles east of Vernal, Utah. It was a portion of Ute land the government had recently opened for settlement. When Josie first saw the beauty of the region, with its lush green meadows and quiet solitude, she must have sensed that this land, this place, would be where she would live for the rest of her life. She chose a spot featuring vast open meadow at one end and the base of Blue Mountain, almost like a rock fortress, at the other end. The homestead had natural flowing springs, providing water, and plenty of open space for grazing livestock. Perhaps the most important factor for Josie: The plot sat miles away from land other settlers to the area would claim.

When the lease on the Davenport ranch came up in the fall of 1913, Josie and Ben Morris pulled up stakes in Browns Park and headed for Utah and the homestead. Herding fifty head of cattle and fifty sheep, they crossed over Blue Mountain and followed Green River to the homestead along Cub Creek.

On November 24, 1913, not long after settling at their new place, Josie Bassett McKnight Ranney Williams Wells married the known sheep thief Ben Morris in Jensen, Utah. Shortly after the marriage ceremony, the couple found a place near Jensen to hold their stock throughout the winter.

No sooner had Josie begun clearing her land for improvements than she faced obstruction from a neighboring foe. Josie's nearest neighbor, Benjamin Daniels, who had inherited his land from his father, filed a lawsuit against her over the water rights to the land. The case went to court, where a jury awarded the Cub Creek water rights to Daniels. Nonetheless, Josie maintained water rights to the many flowing springs on her property. Daniels and his attorney warned her that should those springs overflow into Cub Creek, they would be considered tributaries to the creek, which Daniels could claim. In light of this threat, an obstinate Josie would flood her own meadowlands each spring season before she let any water drain into Cub Creek.

In the spring of 1914, Josie and her husband, Ben, cleared brush, built a corral for the cattle, and built chicken coops. The sheep grazed in the open meadow. Josie planted a large vegetable garden as well as saplings of apple, apricot, and plum trees, the beginnings of what she hoped would be a fine orchard. Josie and Ben lived in a tent that first summer as Ben built two small but adequate cabins. Built side by side and facing the ridge of Blue Mountain, the cabins were intended for the Morris couple and Josie's father, Herb Bassett, when he came to visit. Not long after the cabins were built, the Morrises received their first visitor. Josie's sister, Ann, arrived for a much-needed vacation after being acquitted for the second time of cattle rustling in Browns Park. Ann was just as taken with the area as her sister was and purchased a proved-up claim on South Fork, approximately five miles from her sister's place, across Cub Creek. Ann settled in at her new ranch in Utah for a time. When Herb Bassett finally came to visit his daughter, he stayed at the cabin Josie and Ben had built for him and helped build a small cabin for Ann on her new property. The ever flighty Ann soon became bored and would leave the ranch to travel for extended periods of time. As Josie would later say, "Ann could never be satisfied if it were too long a ride to town."

After two years of marriage, the well-mannered, easy-going Josie became impatient with her husband's crude behavior. When Josie caught Ben mistreating a horse, she finally had enough. Ben had used a spade bit on a feisty horse in an effort to control the animal. Furious, Josie rushed to the horse, whose mouth had been injured and was now dripping with blood.

Enraged, Josie ran to the cabin and returned with a frying pan, waving it at Ben to get him off her property. An astonished Ben immediately

Josie at her ranch at Cub Creek, Utah

left. When a neighbor asked what had happened, Ben replied, "She gave me fifteen minutes to get off her property, and I only used five of them." Josie eventually went to Jensen, Utah, and filed for divorce. Hi Bernard, Josie's former brother-in-law, would later say, "Josie Bassett McKnight is a jolly good natured woman, she works like a steam shovel and then she hunts up some unworthy bums and gives away the proceeds of her labor. Her hobby is husbands. She has had five or six good men and discards them one after the other without a backward glance."

Following the divorce, Crawford came over Blue Mountain to help his mother. Crawford now living with her, Josie saw an opportunity to expand her homestead. In early 1915 she proposed Crawford file on a homestead up on Blue Mountain. This would give them grazing rights so they could also expand the cattle herd. Mother and son worked well together, and Josie was finally happy and content with her life.

A year later Crawford met the love of his life at a dance in Jensen. Flossie Murray was a member of one of the area's many prominent Mormon families. Her paternal grandparents, Jeremiah Hatch Murray and Karen Maria Nilsson Murray, emigrated to Salt Lake City, Utah, on foot as members of the famed "Handcart Brigade." Her maternal grandfather, Nathan Hunting, was the first bishop of the Mormon church in Jensen, Utah.

When pretty eighteen-year-old Flossie met handsome twenty-three-year-old Crawford, it was instant love for her as well. Their ensuing courtship, however, met with disapproval from Flossie's parents. Jensen was a Mormon town with strict moral values. The very idea that Crawford McKnight came from the notorious area of Browns Park, and that his mother divorced not one but three husbands, was a shocking revelation the Murray family had difficulty overcoming.

On the other hand, Crawford's family welcomed Flossie with open arms. Josie instantly liked her, and Crawford's aunt Ann drove Flossie over Blue Mountain to meet Ann's father and brothers. Flossie enjoyed spending time with the Bassett family and told her parents all about them when she returned home. When the Murrays voiced their objections, their strong-willed daughter countered by telling them of her time spent with Crawford's grandfather, Herb, who talked about religion with her just as she had heard religion spoken about in their own church in Jensen. The defiant Flossie continued to see Crawford over her parents' objections.

Then America entered World War I. In 1917 Crawford was drafted into the United States Army. Despite the resistance of her parents, Flossie and Crawford married the day before he left to formally enlist. After seeing her husband off, Flossie went to Josie's place on Cub Creek rather than live with her disapproving parents. When Crawford sent word that he was stationed in Washington state, Flossie left Josie to join her husband. Now truly alone for the first time, Josie was forced to fend for herself. With the nation at war and her son involved in it, Josie kept herself busy. When her hostile neighbor, Ben Daniels, sold his ranch in 1917, the new owner leased (and would later sell) the ranch to Ed Lewis and his father, a banker from Walsenburg, Colorado.

Ed Lewis, a bachelor, soon introduced himself to his divorced neighbor, Josie. The two soon found they had much in common and began spending considerable time together. Although Josie was some five years older than Ed, the two soon became a couple. It was a perfect relationship for Josie. She lived and worked on her homestead, and Ed lived and worked on his. They spent their free time together. The arrangement worked well for the couple until the end of World War I.

It was during this time that a sad event diverted Josie's attention. On July 30, 1918, her father, Amos Herbert Bassett, died at a veteran soldiers home in Quincy, Illinois. The August 29, 1918 issue of the *Moffat County Mirror* carried his obituary:

*Word was received recently of the death of A. H. Bassett, at the Soldiers Home near Quincy, Illinois. He had been with his daughters, Mrs. Morris and Mrs. Bernard, the past year. In June he went to the soldiers home in Illinois mainly to be under medical treatment for a while. On July 20th he had a severe stroke of paralysis and lived only a few hours. Word failed to reach the family in time, so he was given a military burial at the home. It was not possible for any of his children to be with him when the end came. He leaves five children, Mrs. Josie Morris, Jensen, Utah, Sam Bassett, Alaska, Mrs. Anna M. Bernard, Elbert and George Bassett, Lodore, Colorado.*

Following the war Crawford and Flossie, pregnant with their first child, returned to Cub Creek just in time for the Christmas season. The couple settled into the second cabin, originally built for Josie's father. Crawford immediately began working on the ranch alongside his mother, while Flossie awaited the birth of her child. The living arrangement provided a certain amount of privacy; however, all meals were taken together in the kitchen of Josie's cabin. Although Crawford and Flossie were aware of the relationship between Josie and Ed, Flossie, with her strong Mormon upbringing, became increasingly uncomfortable when Ed was, more often than not, present at the early morning breakfast table. Flossie also began to regret moving back to Cub Creek and life with Josie. She would later say, "Josie was just as good to me as my own mother was, but one kitchen is too small for two strong women."

Ranch life did not suit Flossie, who had always lived in town. Staying at Cub Creek, which was so isolated, became unbearable. Josie seemed to understand her daughter-in-law's feelings. She moved into Ed's cabin to give the young couple privacy. However, every morning she returned to her ranch, where she and Crawford did a full day's work together. The arrangement seemed to work for a time. Within a few months of the birth of her baby girl, Amy, on February 24, 1919, Flossie was again pregnant. Josie tried to give some motherly advice on the subject of contraception, but Flossie felt it was none of her business. Flossie believed preventing pregnancy bordered on sin; she would go on to have five children within eight years. When Flossie went into labor in November 1921, Crawford took her by wagon the five miles to Ed's ranch, where Josie delivered the couple's second child, a healthy boy they named Boon. Less than two years later, in January 1923, Crawford brought his mother back to Cub Creek to deliver their third baby. Josie delivered Belle in the old cabin built for Herb Bassett. By this time the women were barely speaking to each other, and after the baby was born, Josie immediately went back to the Lewis ranch.

During this time Josie and Ed were having difficulties, arguing on a regular basis. Both were strong-willed and hardworking yet possessed enormous tempers. After one particularly heated argument, Josie packed up and moved back to the very crowded cabin on Cub Creek. Flossie was again pregnant. It was clear another cabin would have to be built. Josie and Crawford, along with hired ranch hand Dan Nelson, began building a larger cabin at the base of the box canyon on the property, with a flowing spring nearby.

One day, while clearing land for the new cabin, Josie's skirt became caught in the heavy brush, and Josie could not pull herself free. With a swift, powerful swing of her ax, Josie cut the skirt, freeing herself. She then stormed into the cabin and soon emerged in bib overalls, ready to get back to work. It was a revelation, an awakening for Josie. In the 1920s the new era of social freedom for women who smoked in public, wore flapper dresses, and drank in bars with men was not Josie's new era. Josie had disapproved when her sister began smoking, rolling cigarettes from a pouch of Bull Durham tobacco, and even more so when Ann began drinking whiskey. Imagine Josie's horror when, years later, she would learn that her youngest granddaughter, Betty, routinely stole away into the woods from Josie's cabin to have a smoke from her own pouch of Bull Durham.

Josie's new personal freedom came in wearing trousers. She very simply found it liberating. No longer would she fret over the cumbersome, sweeping skirt. Wearing pants, Josie found herself free and unencumbered when working outdoors. From then on, Josie wore pants wherever she went, except for formal occasions such as weddings and funerals. She sewed her own pants, making them neat and well cut. Another change to Josie's personal appearance occurred during this time. Josie had always worn her long blond hair high on her head. Again, while clearing brush, her hair became entangled on a thorny branch above her. Josie moved

After an incident in which her dress became caught in a patch of heavy brush, Josie wore pants or overalls for the rest of her life.

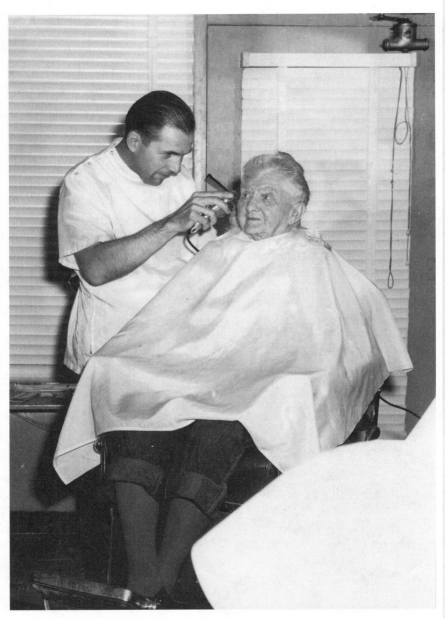

As Josie aged, she kept her hair short.

around, unsuccessfully trying to free her hair, then finally used the ax to cut the branch and free herself. Josie cut her hair off and from then on wore it neat and short. Josie thereby conformed with the new women's era not for the sake of fashion but out of necessity.

Once completed, the new cabin included three bedrooms: one for Crawford and Flossie, one for Josie, and one for the children. It was in this cabin that Josie delivered Flossie's fourth child, Frank, named for Ann's second husband, Frank Willis, in December 1924. The relationship between Flossie and Josie remained strained, and it was an uncomfortable situation for everyone. Crawford was caught in the middle, trying to please his wife and his mother, desperately attempting to keep the peace between the two strong-minded women.

As the new year of 1925 dawned, financial difficulties became a great concern to Josie and Crawford. Crawford had relinquished his land claim on Blue Mountain when he enlisted in the army. Therefore, Josie no longer had the added grazing land and was forced to purchase hay for her cattle during the winter months. This cut into their profit, and Josie experienced economic struggles years before the rest of the country would in the era known as the Great Depression. Whether due to economic necessity or the constant tension between his wife and his mother, Crawford moved his young family to Vernal, Utah, where he obtained gainful employment.

Once again Josie found herself alone. Undaunted, she made the best of her situation. She redecorated her newly built cabin. Josie covered the floors with her hand-braided rugs, spread her quilts over the beds, and hung the mounted heads of a four-point buck and an antelope she had shot years before in Browns Park. In the living room area, Josie placed her mother's hand-painted teacups and finger bowls, which she had brought with her from Arkansas.

Josie was deeply saddened when her younger brother, Elbert "Eb" Bassett, committed suicide in Browns Park in November 1925. The *Craig Courier* ran the following headline in its November 19, 1925 issue: "Lodore Rancher Suicides Eben [sic] Bassett of Browns Park Took Poison at home of Frank Lawrence on Big Gulch early Thursday Morning. Was one of Pioneer Cattlemen of Northwestern Colorado. Was to have

Josie in the kitchen of her Cub Creek cabin

appeared in Court today to answer charge of killing cow." Eb had been involved in a few underhanded dealings and was heavily in debt. In an effort to save the Bassett family ranch, Eb had deeded it to his brother. When Eb was investigated for fraud, a judge ruled that deeding the ranch to George was an effort to hide assets, and Eb lost the family ranch. Josie believed Eb was remorseful for losing the ranch and "just grew tired of living." However, Crawford later said that Eb was in love with a woman "he could never have."

While the factors cited by Josie and Crawford might have played a part in Eb's decision to commit suicide, the *Moffat County Mirror* published an article detailing the circumstances surrounding the event in its November 25, 1925 issue:

### Dies With Boots Off Browns Park Rancher Suicides on Eve of Hearing on Charge of Cattle Theft Court Dismisses Defendants

*"No one but me knows or suspects what I am going to do, no one."*

*(Signed) Eb Bassett.*

*This was the note that led to finding the body of Eb Bassett at the Frank Lawrence ranch on lower Big Gulch last Thursday morning. Bassett, W. E. Sweet and Ed Ainge were on their way to Craig to appear before Justice of the Peace W. C. Held on a charge of killing cattle and misbranding a horse and decided to spend the night at the Lawrence ranch. After the evening meal Bassett led the conversation to the subject of poisoning coyotes and on being told that there was a small package of strychnine crystals on the place asked to see them as he said that he had always used the powdered form. The box was brought forth and passed around after which it was placed on the table in the room that Bassett was to occupy for the night. Mr. and Mrs. Sweet were in one room while Bassett and Lawrence slept together a bed in the kitchen with Ainge in a bed on the floor by their side. It was noticed that Bassett was missing when the others rose in the morning but nothing was thought of the matter until the note was found and this led to the discovery of the body in one of the outbuildings. The body was brought to Craig at once and an inquest and autopsy was held with the verdict "died from taking poison into his stomach." Bassett was a real pioneer of this section, having made Brown's park [sic] his home since childhood. He had been engaged in the cattle business all his life and enjoyed a wide acquaintance over the west. He was a brother of the famous Queen Anne who took much space on the front pages of newspapers shortly after Routt county [sic] was divided. The trial was one of the first in the then new county, Moffat, and it took the greater part of five days to find her not guilty which event was celebrated by street parades and other demonstrations.*

Ann had received the nickname "Queen" from the Craig newspapers, which covered her cattle rustling trials. Queen Ann was acquitted in both trials.

Following Eb's death, Josie went to Browns Park, where she and George held a small service for Eb and buried him in the Bassett family cemetery. Eb had left his few assets, mostly cattle, to his sisters. As Ann was in California with her husband, Frank Willis, it was left to Josie to round up what was left of Eb's cattle. She arrived in Zenobia Basin in Browns Park on a chilly November day. As she gathered the cattle for the long trip back to Cub Creek, a few local ranchers watched and checked that none of the animals had their brands. Josie realized Eb's reputation in the Park was not a good one. Years later, George Bassett's daughter, Edna, would remark on the bond between the brothers:

*As far back as my knowledge goes, Eb did many things, terrible things, that were extremely hurtful and expensive, dad seemed to take it all stoically, trying to smooth things over, make amends. They were friends, they worked together some, saw a good deal of each other, and I know Dad was fond of Eb, making it that much harder for him to bear Eb's transgressions.*

Dispirited, Josie drove the cattle to her Cub Creek ranch, where she was again alone. Yet she wasted no time feeling sorry for herself. She managed to keep up the operation of her ranch. Josie also built a new cabin with the help of her grandson Frank. She installed large windows and used concrete for the floors. The fireplace would serve as the sole source of warmth in the cold winter months. The kitchen was adequate for Josie's needs, although she would still haul fresh water from the spring.

To supplement her income, Josie began making her own brandy and whiskey. This was quite uncharacteristic, as she had always detested alcohol. However, the circumstances had changed. Prohibition law had ruled for the past few years. Josie was experiencing financial constraints but had a fine fruit orchard: She decided to take advantage of the situation. She erected a still, supplied by her brother-in-law, Frank Willis, in a gulch not far from her cabin. Here she brewed corn whiskey and several varieties of brandy, using fruit from her orchard for the latter. Josie enjoyed the brewing process, which Willis had taught her, and took pride in her recipes. She was particularly proud of her apricot brandy, even sampling a bit for herself from time to time.

Josie sold her mountain moonshine to area ranchers, using the profits from her enterprise to cover ranch expenses. Josie also donated some of the proceeds to neighbors in need. It was the era of Prohibition and the Great Depression, and Josie felt it her duty to help her neighbors. Josie also supplied food, particularly beef, to others in the area. This remote region of Utah suffered a particularly depressed economy. Many suspected Josie's generosity came from illegal means, but no one said anything. Josie's friends and neighbors were grateful for her generosity and looked out for her as well. When family and friends warned Josie that government revenue agents were looking for her still, she destroyed it.

Then, in January 1936, a local rancher and bitter adversary, James "Jim" Robinson, accused Josie of rustling his cattle, butchering them, and selling the beef to local families. Robinson and Josie had formerly been partners of a sort. For a time Robinson had used Josie's ranch as his headquarters when grazing sheep nearby. Then the two had engaged in a heated argument, and Josie threw him off her land. They remained enemies ever after.

A few years later Josie and her granddaughter Belle rode over Blue Mountain to visit a rancher. Their path brought them near land belonging to the Chew family, dear friends of the Bassetts. Robinson, who was married to one of the Chew daughters, was staying there. At a point near Red Rock Canyon, Robinson, concealed in the brush, yelled at Josie and Belle, accusing them of trespassing and demanding they turn back. Josie would have none of it, explaining that they were on a public road and public land. Neither Josie nor Belle could see Robinson; however, they saw he brandished an object. Josie thought it was a stick, but Belle saw a shining spot reflected by the sunlight. Sure it was a rifle or shotgun, Belle turned her horse around and told her grandmother to follow her. Whether it was a gun or stick, Josie felt they may have been in serious danger. Later she filed a complaint with the county sheriff. After a court hearing, where Josie and Belle testified, the judge placed a restraining order on Robinson, prohibiting him from confronting or harassing Josie and her family. Josie and her family believed this latest allegation of cattle rustling was just another stunt fueled by Robinson's vindictiveness against Josie. Nevertheless, Josie was eventually indicted for cattle rustling. Robinson's complaint alleged that the hides of his animals could be found on Josie's land. Josie immediately sensed a setup, just as Ann had faced in her trial in 1913 for the same crime. Just as Ann had been, Josie also would be tried twice for the same alleged act.

A posse of men rode over to Josie's ranch in search of evidence. Included in this group were Andrew Dudley, Elmer and Newel Snow, Harley Wilkins, and incredibly, the accuser, Jim Robinson. Also included in the posse were Robinson's son-in-law, Deputy Sheriff Frank Swain, and his brother, Garn Swain, as well as the Uintah County attorney, Hugh Colton. Colton would later recount the incident:

> *There was an old boy named Jim Robinson who was tainted with the past along the lines. . . . He married one of the Chew girls, which is quite a family too. He ran a bunch of sheep at this time, although he was an old-time cowboy, and leased a homestead as kind of a headquarters. They had quarreled, Josie and he, and he had squealed on her. He went to people in Jensen who ran their cattle on Blue Mountain and said, "Josie's been stealin' beef." The sheriff investigated, and she had delivered six in the last three months or so to this meat*

*shop. It looked like a good case, and it was. So we talked it over and Elmer Snow decided that we should get a search warrant for her place. Everything was legal. We got to Jensen and here were six of these people who had missed cattle. Way back then we had nothing but a Model T Ford. The fellows were all ready, they came out with rifles. We asked what this was for, and Jim Robinson said, "Well, she's a dangerous woman." So we went up the east side of Cub Creek—there's a ridge there about a quarter-mile from Josie's cabin. They stop and dismounted, and I said to the deputy, "What's this for?" "Well, we don't want her to get the drop on us." I think it was probably Jim Robinson who had 'em all spooked, saying, "She'll shoot you if she sees you coming." Finally I said to the deputy, "What the heck goes on here? Let's go down and talk to her." He said, "That's the way I feel." The deputy and I walked down [to the ranch]. She said, "Good morning gentlemen, how are you? Won't you come in and have a cup of coffee?" So we did. She served us coffee and we talked, and finally Frank said, "Well Jose [sic], we got some bad news for you. We've got a search warrant here and you've been accused of butchering cattle." She took the paper and asked what she could do to help out, just as cooperative as a person could be. She said, "Well how do you want to do it?" Then, for the first time, she got a little sarcastic and she said, "Why don't those others come down here with you?" They were lying up there on the hill, thinking they were hiding from her, and she had known everything that was going on! She said, "Especially this Jim Robinson—if there's anything here, he did it."*

Josie proceeded to tell the posse she had indeed butchered three cows the previous summer and sold them to a butcher shop in Vernal, Utah. However, as the men canvassed her property, Jim Robinson instructed them exactly where to dig for the evidence. Eight hides in various states of decay were dug up from the frozen January ground. Curiously, each hide had been rolled into a small, tight bundle that included wild hay, which Josie readily admitted was from her haystack about fifty yards from where the hides had been found. The evidence was transported to the Newton Company, a dealer in hides, for verification of brands.

Hugh Colton continued his account of the posse at Josie's ranch:

*Her profession—her trade—had been making moonshine, and there was a little log cabin maybe a fourth the size of a room, with a sloping roof and room for a still and a couple of barrels to brew her mash in. On top of the roof were some cleats, and over these there was a cow hide covered with willows, and with dirt shoveled on to keep the willows down, just to make a shelter. Robinson had been a neighbor, living and running his sheep right in that area, and he knew all about it and he told them what to expect. We found a bull whip, maybe twenty feet long with a long handle of braided rawhide. They were used a lot in the old days in driving cattle, and the cowboys became expert. Josie said, "Well! I wondered where that was," and picked it up . . . she carried it with her [and] was becoming less talkative as we went along. She knew she was caught. Josie was still carrying this bull whip. As we started digging those eight hides out of the gulch she let that bull whip go. And she popped that thing—it sounded just like a revolver. Then she lit into this Jim Robinson and said, "And you're the dirty so and so who turned in this whole story to these people. You're the one who buried these hides. You haven't got guts enough to come close enough that I can reach you or I'd cut your blankety-blank throat." I think she could have done too, she could throw that bull whip and make it sound just like a gun. I can remember her just like it was yesterday, poppin' that whip at this guy. And he didn't come close, and he didn't say "That isn't true." She was very definitely in a rage and she knew all the words. Then she told something about his life history with the Chews, in the presence of all these men. When she got over her rage she cooperated in every way. The deputy said, "Well Josie, we'll have to take you into town." And she agreed, saying, "Do you mind if I change clothes?" Somebody piped up and said, "Yeah, and get a gun?" Frank said, "Look, I'll handle this," because she didn't show one act of hostility to any of us except Jim Robinson. So she*

*came out after she changed her clothes and had fed her chickens again,*
*because she wouldn't be back that night; and we took her to town and*
*took her to the J. P. and filed a criminal complaint. The J. P. gave her a*
*preliminary hearing and bound her over to the District Court."*

Josie's bail was paid by local ranchers, including her onetime lover
Ed Lewis, and Josie immediately hired an attorney, Wallace Calder, who
was also the president of the local branch of the Mormon Church. After
hearing Josie's story, he was convinced of her innocence and Robinson's
having framed her. When the brand inspections were completed, the
prosecuting attorneys, including Hugh Colton and District Attorney
Marcellus Pope, went forward with the charges against Josie. They based
their case on an ostensible match between one partial hide and another
piece of hide the posse members had found hanging over Josie's fence.
They made this case despite Josie's having explained at the time of the
raid that the hide came from a cow belonging to local rancher Henry
Rasmussen, for whom she said she had butchered the cow. She had further explained that the remainder of the hide on the fence had been used
for rawhide strips and lariats by her grandson Boon.

When the trial began the following month, sixty-two-year-old Josie
arrived arrayed in a fine dress, looking very much like a gray-haired
grandmother. Hugh Colton would later describe the trial and Josie's
actions:

*The day of the trial was set and in walks Josie. She said, "Good*
*morning, Judge," smiling in her gracious way, a very gracious, gray-*
*haired lady. I think we were three days presenting the evidence. Each*
*morning she would walk into the court room and first turn to the*
*jurors. "Good morning, ladies and gentlemen." Then, "Good morning,*
*Judge; Good morning, Mr. Pope," and then say "Good morning" to*
*me. She would sit there, a pleasant woman, and here we were, in the*
*back of our minds always thinking how distasteful it was to accuse*
*a lady as gracious-appearing as she was of stealing cattle, which is a*
*penitentiary offense. But I mean, we worked at it. Because this whole*
*community makes a living on livestock and the whole community*

*was wrapped up in it. We thought we had a cinch case. But we had one person from Jensen, a man on the jury, whom we had thought would be a cinch, principally because he knew all these men. I guess they deliberated maybe five, six hours, and came in with a hung jury, and investigation showed that this neighbor down there—his name was Joe Paulson—had led all the opposition. Well, then the district attorney said, "Something's wrong here, we're going to try her again." And we did. We went through the same thing, only this time she was perhaps a little more pleasant, each morning as she came to court. This time we were real careful about choosing a jury, because it was a cinch case. We went through that whole thing again for two or three days, and we argued a little more convincingly to the jury, we thought, about the facts of the case, to where there should have been no question that she was guilty—and there wasn't. So we wait for the jury again, and they come in a second time with a hung jury. It was about evenly split—I don't know who led the opposition, and frankly didn't care. After the trial Mr. Pope said, "Well, we'll just have to try again," and I said, "Look, here's this old lady, and we've done the best we can with two juries. And she's beat us. Let's be sports enough to forget it." He said, "I agree with you," so we didn't try her again. But this is keeping with her nature and disposition. She had to be a very smart woman."*

Years later Josie, perhaps with a chuckle and a wink in her eye, spoke about the trial: "I put on a frilly dress, wore sensible shoes, and had my hair done in a domestic style on the top of my head. I looked like a petite little grandmother as I stood before the judge. I said to the judge and the jury, 'Your Honor, do you seriously believe that a little old lady could kill and butcher out even one beef cow by herself?'"

A little over a year later, Josie walked into the offices of District Attorney Marcellus Pope and Hugh Colton, who had prosecuted and lost his cases against Josie. Colton would later recall the incident:

*Some time later she walked into my office and said, "Good morning Mr. Colton." I hadn't seen her since the trial, but she couldn't help but know that I had done everything I could to convict her. I was then,*

Josie Morris in her Cub Creek home

*and still am, in the cattle business and I was concerned about this. So she greeted me very cordially and said, "I want to ask you a question. I want to know if you would represent me in a case, and work as hard for me as you did against me in that cow-stealing case?" I looked at her and laughed and said, "What do you think?" She said, "I think you will." I answered her, "Well you can be assured I will." And I did. The facts in the matter are these: At the time she had a neighbor, Harry Aumiller, who had employed her. He had about twenty or thirty horses to winter, and he had these stacks of hay, and asked her to feed these horses during the winter, which she agreed to. Aumiller spent his winters in Jensen. And that old lady—that was one of the hardest winters here, and the snow was so deep that from January until the next April, no one even saw her—that old lady stood out there and shoveled the snow off these haystacks which is a hard job—and fed those horses. Along in April they got worried about her, and her grandson Boon flew over and saw her forking hay to those horses. He waved at her and she waved back. When spring came she said, "I want my money," and he said, "Well I'll see about it," and wouldn't pay her. So she came in and had me represent her in suing him that winter's work. I thought at first that he would pay it without any question, because she was right—she had it coming and more too. Anyway, he didn't pay her, so we sued and got a judgment against him. He was kind of thumbing his nose at her, saying, "Try and get it." So that was my job again. I waited until he had a bank account big enough to pay it, and executed on it, and got her the money. Thank God! I never handled a case that pleased me quite so much as to make this guy trying to beat this old woman pay her."*

Meanwhile, Josie remained estranged from her younger son, Chick. Chick had always remained fond of and loyal to his Aunt Ann. Not long after Ann's marriage to Frank Willis in 1923, the couple moved to California, where Frank worked in the oil fields for Richfield Oil Company and Ann ran the Cooper Hotel in Huntington Beach. Chick had lived in California for some time and even worked as a stunt rider in Hollywood movies. In 1928 Chick and his wife, Edith, joined Ann and Frank in Huntington Beach. During their time in California, Ann and Frank received a visit from an old friend of Ann. Edith McKnight, Josie's daughter-in-law, whom Josie had never met, would later recall the occasion:

*Queen Ann was running a little rooming house for the oil workers at Huntington Beach, California. Chick and I were running a riding academy over near Hermosa Beach. Ann called and asked us to come down the next weekend. She mentioned Elza Lay was coming to visit and bringing his wife and children along, too. Chick and I went to Ann's place. Elza, his wife [Mary] and two children [James and Mary Lucille], were already there. They were well dressed and very pleasant to visit with. I have to admit, I was never around nicer people. Elza didn't look like a bank robber. His appearance was more that of a banker.*

In 1931 Ann and Frank purchased a cattle ranch at Hackberry, Arizona, and Chick and Edith joined them. The two couples worked as partners in the ranch operations. Over time it became a fairly successful ranch, with twelve hundred head of cattle. However, approximately eighteen months later, Chick was involved in a terrible automobile accident. With his neck broken in three places, he was out of commission for the next two years. This was the height of the Great Depression, and the Willis ranch was already struggling financially. Under these circumstances, Chick's absence forced Frank and Ann to sell out in 1937.

During his convalescence, Chick corresponded with his mother. In one of the letters, he writes of his injury and the economic hardships:

*Your letter was rather an agreeable surprise. Edith and I are getting along fairly well. She is boarding some men and I am working at a job where I don't have much to do. I haven't much use of my left arm and no strength in either of them but my neck is growing back in fairly good shape. Wish you would come down here. I think you would like this country. Down where Ann is it's a desert, the worst part of the country, but back over in the part Edith and I are in there is plenty of water and its very good cow country. I didn't get much done when I got hurt. Got a good house built but no fencing or anything else done. What we need is some cattle but I don't see how we are going to get them now. Cattle are sure cheap now if a fellow could just get some money. This would be a fine chance to buy some and they won't always stay down. Good cows sold here last fall for a cent a pound.*

One wonders whether, after years of silence between mother and son, Chick was subtly asking his mother for financial help. In time he eventually recovered, and he and Edith relocated to Fallon, Nevada, where they operated a small ranch.

Meanwhile, Josie spent several years in quiet solitude on her ranch. For the first time she may even have enjoyed being independent and living alone. Her grandchildren came every summer, which must have been a joy to the aging lady rancher. During World War II, Josie finally became a respectable member of the predominately Mormon community. She often took meat, fruit, and clothing to those in need.

Yet the war had taken an economic toll on many of the farmers and ranchers, including Josie. Not long after the war ended in 1945, seventy-one-year-old Josie applied for a bank loan, but she was turned down, most likely due to her age. Strong-willed Josie would not be deterred from her plans to increase the size of her cattle herd and thereby improve her economic situation. Unfortunately, she fell victim to a land scheme of sorts. To fund her plan, Josie chose to deed her land to a young rancher who could qualify for a loan. Josie signed over her land and expected the assignee to get the loan they had agreed on. However, Josie was in for the shock of her life.

Six months after Josie deeded her property to the young rancher, he in turn sold the note to none other than Harry Aumiller, the very man Josie had taken to court for nonpayment of services rendered. A week later, Aumiller, who must have been gloating in his payback, leased Josie's land to a horse rancher. Josie was enraged. She was not about to lose her land to anyone, let alone Harry Aumiller. Josie saddled her horse, packed her rifle, and rode to Vernal. A very sympathetic sheriff calmed her down and, acknowledging her outrage and frustration, explained that nothing could be done. Crawford, Flossie, and a few of the children accompanied her back to Cub Creek.

As it turned out, Josie realized that Utah public lands were divided among a myriad of government bureaucracies, including the Bureaus of Indian Affairs and Land Management and the National Park Service. There were also Utah state lands, including "school lands." The last cabin Josie had built stood on what was considered Utah "school land." In a twist of fortune for Josie, the state of Utah put up that piece of land for sale. Crawford bought the five-acre plot and deeded it over to his mother.

Although Josie had lost most of her land, she was able to hang on to the bit that had not been swindled from her. She lived modestly in her cabin, but then again she had always lived modestly. Friends and neighbors often wondered how she acquired the beef she slaughtered and sold, but no one said anything, for she was also very generous to her neighbors. In her own way, Josie was able to support herself.

## Chapter Six

# The End of an Era

IN JANUARY 1948 *LIFE* MAGAZINE RAN A FEATURE ARTICLE ON JOSIE. Ann and her husband were visiting at the time of the interview and took Josie to Vernal. If Ann envied the national attention Josie would soon receive for her life as a lady rancher, she never let on. The *Life* magazine editor even mentioned that the story could possibly become a Hollywood movie. Now the sibling rivalry that had always existed between the sisters simmered in Ann. At a photo shoot for the article, the sisters' appearances struck a stark contrast: Ann dressed in high fashion, and Josie wore overalls, a felt hat, and tennis shoes. Josie had been told, and Ann had not, that the photo shoots would feature Josie on horseback, photos of her with a shotgun, and photos of her shooting. Obviously, it was Josie and not Ann who had dressed for the part. When the article entitled "Queen of the Rustlers" was published, Ann grew enraged. Not to be outdone, Ann would later write her own version of life in Browns Park, eventually published by the Colorado Historical Society.

Where the sibling rivalry was concerned, Josie would get the last laugh when Hollywood made a film loosely based on her life. Released in 1967, *The Ballad of Josie* starred Doris Day as the lady rancher. It was nothing close to Josie's life but made for good box office receipts.

Meanwhile, the *Life* magazine article garnered Josie much publicity. Teachers brought their students out to her ranch, where Josie would captivate her young audience with lively stories and tours. In Maybell, Colorado, southeast of Browns Park, a women's group often hosted Josie, touting her as one of Colorado's pioneer women. In keeping with the

Josie crossing the river at Browns Park

pioneer theme, Jay Searle, president of Vernal's roping club, enticed Josie, with a swank rodeo outfit and a brand-new saddle, to be the rodeo queen in the club's annual rodeo. At the age of seventy-nine, Josie sat astride a fine pinto and galloped around an arena waving her hat at a cheering crowd. Josie even participated in a horse race and finished in third place. Josie showed no sign of slowing down.

However, later that same year, Josie did experience a setback. The mortar around her fireplace was crumbling, eventually causing a fire. Josie would later say, "If it had happened to anybody but me, they most assuredly would have cried."

A letter addressed to Josie's dear friends Duard and Esther Campbell and dated January 1954 recounted the incident:

*After a long time I am going to try and answer your nice and welcomed letter. I have been full of business and not in the notion to write. I got my metal fireplace but have had some things to think about. I had a fire in my house and it left me a mess, it took the north end of the living room and bedroom, the paper burned and it looks bad, the fire was behind the paper. I took the bar and pulled down the paper, then the flame was on the floor. It got all my best clothes, some pillows, some rugs and so many things I can't mention. I got water from the spring and lost no time throwing it on. I took the wrecking bar and pulled down the burning logs and after hard work and some managing, stopped it. No one hurt bad. I blistered my arms but am all right.*

Josie and Chick had occasionally corresponded over the years. Finally, after nearly forty years, the estranged son and his wife took a trip to Utah, visiting Crawford and his family. From there they made the trip to Cub Creek to see Josie.

When they arrived, there was no one at the cabin. They walked around the grounds for a few minutes, calling out for Josie. Then the door of the storage cellar opened and Josie appeared. She politely greeted the couple and asked what she could do for them. Chick then told Josie who he was. Thrilled and embarrassed at the same time, she embraced her son and invited the pair into her cabin. Chick and Edith stayed a week with Josie, a visit she thoroughly enjoyed.

The Christmas season of 1951 was interrupted by tragedy. Josie's youngest brother, George, suddenly died. George had been the last of the Bassett family to remain in Browns Park, where he had made his living raising purebred Hereford cattle. George was sixty-seven when he died on Sunday, December 23, 1951. The *Craig Empire Courier* newspaper carried the obituary in its December 30, 1951 issue:

### Funeral Services Held For Browns Park Pioneer

*Funeral services for George Bassett, 67, pioneer Browns Park rancher who died Sunday evening, December 23, at his ranch home were conducted Thursday at 10:30 a.m. at the Congregational Church, with the Rev. A. C. Best officiating. During the services Mrs. Tom Blevins furnished musical selections including "The 23rd Psalm," and the "Lord's Prayer." Pallbearers were Boyd Walker, Elbert Walker, Reg Buffham, Roy Templeton, L. H. Buffham and Tom Blevins. Interment was in the family plot on the Bassett ranch in Browns Park, in the afternoon, with Ralph L. White conducting the graveside services. Mr. Bassett's parents, Herbert and Eliza [sic] Bassett came to Browns Park in the early 1870's with the first group of settlers to make their home. They established permanent residence on the place that has since been known as the Bassett ranch. Here George was born, March 28, 1884, the youngest of a family of five. He grew up with the country, enduring the dangers and hardships of a pioneering life. Much of the stirring and colorful history of the early days of the country has been woven around him and other members of his family. During his early youth he became an expert cattleman. His entire lifetime was devoted to that occupation on the ranch of his birth-place. For some time prior to his death he had been engaged in raising purebred Hereford cattle. He married Alma Ruby McClure in July of 1909, and to this union one daughter was born, Georgia Edna. He is survived by his wife, Ruby Bassett; a daughter, Mrs. Paul Haworth, all of Craig; two sisters, Mrs. Josie Morris of Jensen, Utah, and Mrs. Frank Willis of Leeds, Utah.*

In the spring of 1953, Frank and Ann were at their cabin in Browns Park when Ann suffered a severe heart attack. She was airlifted by helicopter to Craig Memorial Hospital. Worried sick over his beloved wife,

Frank never left the hospital. He notified Ann's favorite grandniece, Betty, Josie's granddaughter, who notified her father, Crawford. Crawford brought Josie to Craig from her cabin on Cub Creek. Josie wept as she entered the hospital room where Ann lay near death. Betty and Frank were at the bedside. Of the event, Betty would later say she had never seen her strong, tough grandmother cry. Josie sat by Ann's bed and held her hand for hours.

On May 8, 1956, Ann Bassett Bernard Willis died at her home in Leeds, Utah, just days before her seventy-ninth birthday. Ann's dear friend Esther Campbell provided the *Craig Empire Courier* with an obituary, which was printed in the May 16, 1956 issue:

### Ann Bassett Willis Dies At 79 After Interesting Life

*The following information on Mrs. Willis's life was compiled and submitted to the* Empire-Courier *by Mrs. D. E. Campbell. Mrs. Ann Bassett Willis, who was a former Moffat County resident and who helped make Browns Park History, died at her home in Leeds, Utah, [last] Wednesday evening, three days before her 79th birthday. Mrs. Willis had suffered from a heart ailment for several years. After a severe heart attack in September, 1953, she became a patient at the Craig Memorial Hospital for about three weeks after having spent the summer at her old home in Browns Park. She never fully regained her strength.*

Now Josie was the last of the Browns Park Bassett children. Josie continued to live on her small claim at Cub Creek. She was comfortable in the cabin she had built with her own hands, heated by a recently repaired fireplace. There was no electricity, but Josie didn't need it. She was a rugged pioneer woman and got by with what she had. Her few cattle and chickens and vegetable garden sustained her.

Daun DeJournette had fond memories of visiting Josie at her cabin around this time. She would later write:

*I remember the first time I saw Josie. It was the Vernal Rodeo in 1956. I was twenty-seven years old. We were sitting in the bleachers, and I was up just one row higher than Josie. My thoughts immediately centered on Josie rather than the rodeo. I was thinking of the stories and rumors about Josie. I remembered Dick's mother, Rosalie [Miles], telling me of her friendship with Queen Ann and Josie. She was well acquainted with both of them. I studied the fine features of her face and realized she was a very petite woman. She had overalls and a cowboy shirt on. She was dressed more like a cowboy heading for the range. I remembered Rosalie telling about her beautiful thick hair and I found myself wondering what she would look like in a dress. Rosalie had been wanting me to take her to see Josie for quite a while. I decided that was exactly what I wanted to do. It was early afternoon and Rosalie and I were on our way to my first visit with Josie. She lived northeast of Jensen, Utah. We went down a really steep red-clay dugway. I thought, "Boy, I'd hate to travel this road during a rainstorm." There wasn't a bridge across Cub Creek then, so we drove right through the water in the creek. We went around a bend, and we could see Josie's cabin nestled among the rugged rocks with jagged edges. The huge rocks looked like twisted rainbow spirals reaching toward the sky. Her little palomino mare grazed in a grassy pasture, surrounded by fruit trees loaded with fruit. Josie opened the door and greeted us with a pleasant smile. Near her cabin was a clear little spring where she kept her milk and butter cool. She invited us in and I was fascinated by her cabin. The surroundings and pleasant aroma of cooking made it seem very cozy. The black and white dog greeted us, but also let us know we were not to harm his mistress.*

At the close of the 1950s, Josie felt her health was suffering. A neighbor took her to the hospital, where she was diagnosed with a bleeding ulcer. While in the hospital, she fell out of bed and broke her collarbone. After some time recuperating in the hospital, a stubborn Josie insisted on going home to Cub Creek. She resumed her work on the ranch, although her right hand plagued her a bit.

For years newspaper reporters and curious writers had often made their way to Cub Creek to interview Josie. Many were interested in her life and her time at Browns Park, particularly after the sensational book

Josie Bassett as Queen of the Vernal Rodeo in 1952
THE MUSEUM OF NORTHWEST COLORADO-CRAIG

*Outlaw Trail: The Story of Butch Cassidy*, by Charles Kelly, was published in 1938. She usually shooed them off her land. Josie would later say of Kelly, "When Kelly dies and goes to hell, the Devil will shun his company for lying about the dead."

Daun DeJournette later recalled that the subject of Kelly came up during one of her visits with Josie. DeJournette wrote: "At one point in the conversation, I had to chuckle under my breath. Josie said, 'It's too bad I'm so damned old, or I'd go after that stinkin' Charles Kelly. Kelly told too many lies in *The Outlaw Trail* like Butch [Cassidy] gettin' bumped off in South America.'"

However, when G. E. Untermann, curator of the Vernal museum, came to visit, Josie agreed to meet with him. He had known her brother George and spent considerable time with him. She talked freely of her life at Browns Park and Cub Creek. At the age of eighty-five, Josie still had a very sharp mind. When Untermann introduced Josie to Murl Messersmith of Dinosaur, Utah, she agreed to a series of taped interviews. Messersmith even took her to Browns Park, where she guided him to a number of sites, such as the old Bassett ranch, the cabin where she had lived during her marriage with Jim McKnight, the first schoolhouse at Vermilion Creek, the site of her uncle Sam's cabin, and various graves that dotted the area, including the Bassett family cemetery.

Josie still planted a garden every spring and made jam, jellies, and pies. She canned the remaining fruits and most of the vegetables and kept them in her storage cellar, which boasted a new roof she herself had put on. She still had her faithful mare, "Old Helen," and several chickens, turkeys, and geese. When neighbors came to visit, Josie always made sure they left with a gift, be it a jar of jam, a homemade pie, or a basket of fresh eggs.

Daun DeJournette recalled the last visit she and her mother-in-law, Rosalie Miles DeJournette, had with Josie at her Cub Creek cabin:

*This was probably the last visit we had with Josie. As we got in the car, Rosalie said, "Josie has been my friend for many years." I glanced at Dick's mother, and I could see a tear sliding down her cheek. Her thoughts were her own and as we drove down the windy road, my*

Rosalie Miles DeJournette was a good friend from Josie's Browns Park days.

*eyes clouded slightly with tears. I'd had the privilege to witness a spe-
cial relationship between two old friends.*

As the years went by, Frank Willis's health declined. Finally, at Josie
and Crawford's urging, Frank agreed to move into a nursing home.
Crawford personally took his uncle to Craig. There he moved Frank
into the Moffat Rest Home, where he could get proper care and medical attention. When Crawford returned to his home, he began cleaning
the cabin Frank had occupied for the past several years, following Ann's
death. Crawford discovered a note nailed to the cabin wall. Written in
Frank's hand, the note read: "To my friends and neighbors everywhere.
My wish is that when I die is to be buryed [sic] on the top of the hill N.
W. of my cabin. I want a plain wooden coffin made by me or some of my
friends. I do not want any undertaker to touch me or have anything to
do with my body. Artificial work does not appeal to me. Frank Willis."
On Tuesday, July 16, 1963, Francis "Frank" Willis died at the age of
seventy-nine. The *Craig Empire Courier* printed the obituary in its July
25, 1963 issue:

### Graveside Services Held Sunday For Frank Willis

*Graveside services were held at the Browns Park Cemetery Sunday
at 2:00 p.m. for Francis (Frank) Willis, 79, with the Reverend Ella
Beyer of the Maybell Congregational Church officiating. Mr. Willis
died Tuesday, July 16th, at the Moffat Rest Home in Craig after
failing health of several years. Surviving Mr. Willis is one daughter
Sister Mary Elene Willis of St. Euphrasia School of Batesburg, South
Carolina.*

Josie and a few of the McKnight grandchildren—all adults by this
time and a few having children of their own—made the trip to Browns
Park for the funeral and burial of Frank Willis. Before the funeral Josie
held a brief family meeting. She was adamant that following Frank's
burial, a small service and burial for Ann's remains would also take place.

Following Ann's death in 1956, her ashes had been sent to Frank from the crematorium in Salt Lake City. Although Ann had requested her ashes be scattered over "her beloved birthplace of Browns Park," for whatever reason Frank could not bring himself to scatter the ashes of his beloved wife. For the next seven years, Frank carried his wife's remains in the trunk of his car. It is unclear whether Josie was aware of this, though it seems likely she was; otherwise, she would have questioned why a burial service for her sister had not occurred. On the other hand, it is hard to imagine that Josie would say and do nothing while her sister's remains were so disrespected.

Nevertheless, the burial of Frank Willis took place according to his wishes. He was buried on a small hill in Browns Park Cemetery, not far from his cabin. Following the funeral, Josie and her family rode over to the Bassett family cemetery, where Josie presided over the solemn burial of Ann's remains. Satisfied that her sister was finally at peace, Josie shed no tears. Wishing to preserve her sister's tranquility into the future, Josie adamantly refused to erect a marker for her sister's grave site, fearing looting or vandalism. This was Josie's way of paying respect to the sister with whom she had fought all her life but whom she truly loved.

Back at her home at Cub Creek, Josie was looking forward to spending Christmas Day 1963 in Jensen with Crawford, Flossie, and the grandchildren. A few days before Crawford was to pick her up, Josie left the cabin to get water from the spring. As she carefully made her way along the icy path, her mare, Old Helen, who always ran loose on the property, came up to Josie and nudged her. Josie lost her footing and fell hard on the ice, her hip hitting the ground first. Josie felt the pain instantly and knew she was seriously injured. Through the dreadful pain, she slowly, inch by inch, pulled herself along the ground back to the cabin. Knowing she would need water, she grabbed her dog's water dish and scraped snow into it. With one hand she pulled the dish while she used the other to drag herself up the porch step and into the cabin. One can only imagine the scene, the fortitude of this strong-minded woman and the sense of survival required for Josie to get herself out of the cold outdoor elements and back to the cabin.

Once inside the warm cabin, where she had previously started a roaring fire, Josie managed to pull the feather-lined covering from the bed. Unable to lift herself onto the feathered bedding, she simply covered herself with it, leaving the dog dish of melting snow near her. It is unknown how long Josie lay there—even Josie was unsure—perhaps one or two nights.

When Crawford and his son, Boon, arrived to bring Josie back to Jensen, Crawford noticed there was no smoke coming from the cabin's chimney. Entering the cabin, he cried out for his mother. He found her on the floor near the fireplace, awake and alert but in great pain. He was hesitant to move her, as he was unsure of her injury. Instead, he built a fire, fed her some soup, and got fresh water from the spring to quench her thirst. Then he went to the nearest neighbor, Robert Smuind, who returned with Crawford to Josie's cabin.

The men were able to shift Josie onto a heavy blanket. Lifting the blanket in a stretcher-like manner, the men managed to get Josie into the vehicle. Returning to Jensen, Crawford and Boon, with the help of Flossie, carried Josie, still on the blanket, into their home. Then Flossie, who had her own personal issues with her mother-in-law, took over in loving fashion. She removed Josie's clothes, washed her soiled body, and dressed her in warm clothing. She, Crawford, and Boon then lifted Josie back into the vehicle and took her to the hospital in Vernal.

The doctors at the Vernal hospital were not encouraging regarding Josie's recovery. After a few days Crawford took her to a hospital in Salt Lake City. There the attending physicians were able to place a pin in her broken hip. After Josie had recuperated from the surgery, Crawford and Flossie brought her back to their home in Jensen.

In time Josie was able to use a walker and soon began to yearn for her cabin at Cub Creek. When Crawford gently explained that she could not return to Cub Creek, Josie, once so strong and independent, began to decline mentally and physically.

By May 1964 Josie was retaining so much fluid that Crawford again took her to the hospital in Salt Lake City. In time Josie began to regain her strength, and she often took long walks along the hospital corridors with the use of her walker. Within a few weeks she was able to leave the hospital. Her granddaughter Belle brought Josie to her home in Salt Lake. Josie seemed to be recovering and continued to gain strength by taking daily walks with her walker. On May 28, 1964, during one of these walks, Josie suddenly fell to the floor and suffered a fatal heart attack. Josephine Bassett McKnight Ranney Williams Wells Morris was dead at the age of ninety.

Crawford and Flossie made arrangements for transportation of Josie's body to a mortuary in Jensen, Utah, where a small service was arranged. However, the bishop of the Jensen Ward of the Mormon Church, the Church of the Latter Day Saints, stepped in and insisted that Josie's funeral should be held in their church. Josie was not a member of the Mormon Church, but she was a pioneer member of the Jensen community.

On Monday, June 1, the funeral service for Josephine Bassett McKnight Ranney Williams Wells Morris drew an overflowing group of mourners, including friends and citizens of Jensen. While many remembered Josie's confrontations with her neighbors and her trials for cattle rustling, they came to pay their respects to the kind woman who had given chickens to a needy family, offered eggs to others, and delivered babies for her neighbors. Held at the Jensen Ward Chapel of the Mormon Church, the service was officiated by Bishop Meril Snow. The bishop related many stories of Josie's generosity and honored the pioneer woman.

Following the service, Vernal Mortuary provided a funeral car for the transportation of Josie's body to Browns Park. Crawford, Flossie, their family, and a long procession of mourners followed the car. As they approached the Bassett family cemetery, on the land where Josie had grown up, the procession was greeted by a large crowd of Browns Park citizens, as well as several Bassett-family friends from Rock Springs, Wyoming. They had come to pay their respects to their friend and the pioneer legend. Burial services were conducted by J. Arben Jolley. The pallbearers were Josie's grandsons and the husbands of her granddaughters, including Nelson Eaton; Jim Lube and his son, Jim Lube, Jr.; Robert Smuin; Larry Wanner; and George McKnight. After a brief ceremony Josie was buried within the iron fencing of the family cemetery, next to

Folks gather at the Bassett ranch in Browns Park for Josie's burial in the family cemetery.

her mother, Elizabeth, and near her sister, Ann. Returning to her childhood home of Browns Park, Josie at last rested in peace with her mother and her sister. Josie was the last of the Bassett pioneers and the last to be buried in the family cemetery at Browns Park.

Days later, an obituary provided by Josie's dear friend Esther Campbell was published in the June 11, 1964 issue of the *Craig Empire Courier*:

> *Browns Park's oldest and most noted pioneer has passed on. Mrs. Josephine Bassett McKnight Morris, one of the last remaining links between the era of the pioneer and the outlaw of early Browns Park history and our present day of progress, died at the home of granddaughter, Mrs. Belle McKnight Christiansen in Salt Lake City, Utah on May 28th. Mrs. Morris was affectionately known by all who knew her as just plain Jose or Josie. She had a multitude of friends and was a friend to all, young and old. Hardly a day passed that visitors didn't come to her isolated home for a friendly visit, some just out of curiosity, some for information of the past. Many writers and historians have received from her the material and facts for newspaper articles, magazines and books telling of her many interesting and exciting*

*experiences. Josie lived a colorful life in a most colorful era. She could ride, rope, shoot and hold her own with the best of them. And until the most recent years, she still rode her old faithful mare Helen, and killed her own venison. Her heart was young and her spirit indomitable. She lived a life of hope.*

It is interesting to note that Josie's old friend Esther, in her kind tribute, referred to Josie as "Mrs. Josephine Bassett McKnight Morris," leaving out her other three married names. The *Craig Empire Courier*, which published the funeral details and obituary on the same day, repeated the reference to Josie as "Mrs. Josephine Bassett McKnight Morris" in their headline for the article. After detailing the burial ceremony, the article provided an edited version of Josie's married life: "She [Josie] married Jim McKnight and they were the parents of two sons, Crawford McKnight of Jensen and Chick McKnight of Aonapa, Nevada. They were divorced and she later married Ben Morris."

This was an obvious attempt by Esther and the newspaper to disregard much of Josie's colorful history, including her many marriages, the divorces, and the suspicion of murder. As Josie had once remarked, "I drove my first husband, Jim McKnight, out of the house at the point of a gun and told him never to come back. Let's just say that some men are harder to get rid of than others."

A smaller article in the same issue of the *Craig Empire Courier*, run under the headline "Funeral Held In Utah for Josie Bassett Morris," listed Josie's survivors and added a few details regarding the funeral service:

*Survivors include two sons, Crawford McKnight of Jensen, Utah, and Chick McKnight of Aonapa, Nevada; eight grandchildren, Boone [sic] McKnight of Jensen, Amy Lube of Vernal, Frank McKnight of Jensen, Betty Eaton of Craig, Dorothy Wanner and Belle Christiansen of Salt Lake City, and Jane Smuin and Wilda McKnight of Jensen; 17 great-grandchildren and 3 great-great-grandchildren. Those from Browns Park and Maybell who joined the friends from Jensen and Vernal at the Bassett Cemetery in Browns Park were Mr. and Mrs. Thomas Blevins, Mr. and Mrs. William Allen and children, Nonie,*

*Diana, Bobbie, and Jerry, Mr. and Mrs. Leslie Allen, Mrs. Lucille Fleming of Green River, Wyoming, Mrs. Arlie Radosevich, Mr. and Mrs. William MacLeod, Mrs. Laura Walker, Mrs. Sam McIntyre, Mr. and Mrs. Elmer Trevenen, and Paul Haworth, and Paul Ellis and other members of the Park Service. She was laid to rest in the little family cemetery on the hill which overlooks the home where she grew from childhood to young womanhood. She has returned to the hills which she roamed and loved. The world is better for the contributions she has made and the life she has given.*

Josephine Bassett McKnight Ranney Williams Wells Morris once reflected on the philosophy of life. Josie said, "You have to keep in action to keep from getting old. I don't intend to let myself get old."

# EPILOGUE

JOSIE'S HOMESTEAD ON CUB CREEK IN UTAH HAS BEEN PRESERVED BY the Bureau of Land Management and is open to the public. Visitors can enter her cabin and imagine what Josie's life was like. Strolling the grounds, one can see why Josie chose such a spot. The meadows are wide and vast and beautiful in the summer. At the other end of the property, the rock formations leading to Blue Mountain are stunning. Not far from Josie's cabin, the chicken coops still remain near one of the free-flowing springs. Around the grounds the Bureau of Land Management has placed interpretive panels amid the many cottonwood trees, describing the location of buildings that stood during Josie's lifetime.

While there are still several ranching operations in Browns Park, a portion of the area is now a National Wildlife Refuge. The refuge is located in a lush valley along the Green River, just north of the Gates of Lodore, the junction of Vermilion Creek and Green River.

Today Josie's cabin and a few outbuildings are preserved at her Cub Creek ranch site.

A portion of Josie's corral still stands.

The author in Josie's cabin at Cub Creek

# Chapter Notes and Source Information

Josephine Bassett agreed to a taped interview, conducted by Murl Messersmith, on July 18, 1960. A second interview was recorded on July 6, 1961, also conducted by Messersmith. The recordings are held in the archives of the Dinosaur National Monument in Jensen, Utah. Quotes attributed to Josie have been drawn from the interviews. Typewritten transcriptions are available at the Museum of Northwest Colorado in Craig, Colorado. Josie's sister, Ann Bassett Bernard Willis, wrote of her life experiences in a four-part series published in the Colorado Historical Society's *Colorado Magazine*. The series, titled "Queen Ann of Browns Park," ran in Volume XXIX January 1952, Volume XXIX April 1952, Volume XXIX October 1952, and Volume XXX January 1953. Copies of the magazine are available at the Denver Public Library. Except where otherwise noted, the quotes attributed to Ann have been drawn from the series.

## Chapter One: The Formidable Years

The records of Private Amos Herbert Bassett are held in the United States National Archives. Copies of his discharge and pension records are available at the Museum of Northwestern Colorado in Craig, Colorado.

The date of Josephine Bassett's birth has been drawn from her obituary, which was provided by her longtime friend Esther Campbell and published in the June 11, 1964 issue of the *Craig Empire Courier*.

The Bassett family first arrived in Brown's Hole in 1877 and subsequently left, returning in 1878. The best source for the early history of Brown's Hole is *Where the Old West Stayed Young* by John Rolfe Burroughs. The Bureau of Land Management's 1982 publication *An Isolated*

*Empire: A History of Northwestern Colorado*, by Frederic J. Athearn, is also quite helpful.

John Rolfe Burroughs's quote regarding cattle rustling can be found on page 56 of *Where the Old West Stayed Young*.

Josie claimed her brother Elbert "Eb" was born in Green River, Wyoming, in 1879, during the Meeker Massacre. According to census records and family history, this is incorrect. It must be remembered that Josie was eighty-six years old when she was interviewed at Dinosaur National Monument.

Ann's descriptions of ranch work were drawn from an excerpt of the partial memoir *Scars and Two Bars* published in the *Moffat County Mirror* in April 1943.

The J. S. Hoy quotes were excerpted from his unpublished manuscript "Early History of Brown's Hole," 1917, courtesy of Valentine Hoy IV. A copy of the manuscript can be found at the Museum of Northwest Colorado.

Hiram "Hi" Bernard's quotes were drawn from "Confidentially Told," an unpublished manuscript written by Frank Willis, Ann Bassett's second husband. Willis spent the summer of 1917 ranging cattle with Bernard near Green River, west of the Bassett ranch. The manuscript is archived at the Museum of Northwest Colorado.

Many of Glade Ross's written recollections are available at the Museum of Northwest Colorado, as well as the Uintah County Library in Vernal, Utah.

Information concerning the outcome of Henry "Harry" Hoy's lawsuit against Elizabeth Bassett and a few of her hired hands comes from court records of the Ninth Judicial District, Colorado, dated 1890. Mary Eliza Chamberlain Miller Bassett was born on August 25, 1855.

Names of Bassett family members buried in the cemetery on the family ranch can be found in Wommack's *From the Grave*.

James "Jesse" S. Hoy's quote regarding the death of Elizabeth Bassett can be found in the J. S. Hoy manuscript at the Colorado History Center.

## CHAPTER TWO: MARRIAGE AND MURDER

"McKnight's Folly" is referenced on page 49 of Grace McClure's *The Bassett Women*. The historic ditch that Josie Bassett McKnight built in 1893 provided water for her lower lands until the construction of Highway 40.

In *The Bassett Women*, McClure refers to the school in Boston as Miss Porter's. It was actually Mrs. Potter's School for Girls, correctly identified in Burroughs' account and Ann's memoirs. During further research, it was learned that the Porter School for Girls, located in Connecticut, has received numerous calls from researchers. Ann Bassett never attended this institution. Further research revealed that several records of Mrs. Potter's School for Girls were burned in a fire.

Esther Campbell, a dear friend to Josie and Ann, wrote about the infamous Thanksgiving dinner, giving the incorrect year.

Matt Warner's quote can be found on page 124 of *Last of the Bandit Riders . . . Revisited*.

The reference to the Josie Bassett McKnight interview with John Rolfe Burroughs can be found on page 165 of *Where the Old West Stayed Young*.

The Crawford McKnight quote regarding the burial site of "Judge" Bennett can be found on page 165 of Burroughs's *Where the Old West Stayed Young*.

Joe Davenport's interview was printed in the March 1, 1929 issue of *Rock Springs Rocket*.

Crawford McKnight's quote regarding his father's reaction to the divorce proceedings can be found on page 68 of *The Bassett Women*.

## CHAPTER THREE: KILLER FOR HIRE

Hiram "Hi" Bernard's quotes were drawn from "Confidentially Told," an unpublished manuscript written by Frank Willis. Willis spent the summer of 1917 ranging cattle with Bernard near Green River, west of the Bassett ranch. Willis married Ann Bassett Bernard in 1923.

While one of Horn's biographers, Larry D. Ball, says Horn's alias was "Thomas Hicks," local newspaper accounts refer to "James Hicks," as do Ann Bassett's memoirs and Browns Park historian John Rolfe Bur-roughs. Grace McClure refers to both "James Hicks" and "Tom Hicks" in her writings. In Josie's taped interview, she refers to him as "Tom Horn" or "Hicks," with no first name. Wallihan quotes can be found on pages 208, 214, and 222 of *Where the West Stayed Young*.

The body of Madison Matthew Rash was taken by family members back to his home state of Texas following a probate case filed by Ann Bassett.

Jesse S. Hoy's concern over the management of Isom Dart's estate was established through Hoy's unpublished manuscript and information shared with the author by his great-grandnephew, Valentine Hoy IV.

### CHAPTER FOUR: WANDERLUST

Crawford McKnight's quote regarding his stepfather, Charles A. Ran-ney, as well as Charles Williams, can be found on page 109 of Grace McClure's excellent work *The Bassett Women*. The letter from Ranney to Josie can also be found in the book.

Bernard's quote regarding Tom Horn can be found in "Confiden-tially Told," Frank Willis's unpublished manuscript.

Richard "Dick" DeJournette's quote regarding his father's recollec-tion of that New Year's Eve event can be found on page 418 of *One Hundred Years of Brown's Park and Diamond Mountain*, by Dick and Daun DeJournette.

Minnie Crouse Ronholdt Rasmussen always maintained that Josie killed her fourth husband. Well into her nineties Rasmussen gave a taped interview, which can be found at the Uintah County Library in Vernal, Utah.

Rasmussen's quote regarding the empty grave can be found on page 153 of *The Romantic and Notorious History of Browns Park*, by Diana Allen Kouris. The quote came from an interview with Kouris's mother, Marie Taylor Allen. Kouris does not give a date for this interview.

Crawford McKnight's quote regarding Minnie Crouse Ronholdt Rasmussen can be found on page 116 of McClure's *The Bassett Women*.

## CHAPTER FIVE: CUB CREEK

Ben Morris's quote can be found on page 124 of Grace McClure's *The Bassett Women*.

Hiram "Hi" Bernard's remark regarding his former sister-in-law was drawn from "Confidentially Told," Frank Willis's unpublished manuscript.

Flossie McKnight's quote regarding her mother-in-law can be found on page 130 of *The Bassett Women*.

Crawford McKnight's assumption regarding the suicide of his uncle Eb Bassett is detailed on page 140 of *The Bassett Women*.

Court records involving Elbert "Eb" Bassett's fraud case can be found in the Moffat County Courthouse. Copies are also held in the archives of the Museum of Northwest Colorado in Craig, Colorado. Many letters of Edna Bassett Haworth, the daughter of Josie's brother George, can be found in the archives of the Museum of Northwest Colorado.

Uintah County attorney Hugh Colton's accounts of the cattle rustling charge against Josie and the subsequent trial are archived in the Uintah County Library in Vernal, Utah.

Josie's remark regarding the cattle rustling charge was drawn from the July 6, 1961 interview conducted by Murl Messersmith. A recording of the interview is available at Dinosaur National Monument in Jensen, Utah.

Edith McKnight Jensen's remembrance of the visit with Elza Lay is detailed in taped recordings in the DeJournette family files. Also see page 332 of DeJournette's *One Hundred Years of Brown's Park and Diamond Mountain*.

## CHAPTER SIX: THE END OF AN ERA

Chick McKnight's letter to his mother can be found on page 165 of McClure's *The Bassett Women*.

Josie's letter to Esther Campbell, dated January 1954, can be found in her letters archived at the Uintah County Library in Vernal, Utah.

Daun DeJournette's recollections of visiting Josie at Cub Creek can be found on page 222 of *One Hundred Years of Brown's Park and Diamond Mountain*.

The last will and testament of Ann Bassett Bernard Willis can be found in the Moffat County Courthouse, and copies are available at the Museum of Northwest Colorado in Craig, Colorado.

Names of Bassett family members buried in the cemetery on the family ranch at Browns Park can be found in Wommack's *From the Grave*.

Mentioned in the funeral notice published in the *Craig Empire Courier*, the Allen family included a young Diana Allen. As a member of the pioneering Allen family of Browns Park, Diana Allen Kouris later wrote *The Romantic and Notorious History of Browns Park*.

# Bibliography

## Primary Sources

Bassett, Josephine. Taped interviews conducted by Murl Messersmith on July 18, 1960, and July 6, 1961. Dinosaur National Monument archives, Jensen, Utah. A typewritten account of the July 18, 1960 interview is available at the Museum of Northwest Colorado, Craig, Colorado.

Campbell, Esther. Notes and correspondence. Uintah County Library, Vernal, Utah.

Hoy, J. S. "History of Brown's Hole," unpublished manuscript. In the possession of Valentine Hoy IV.

Hoy, J. S. "History of Brown's Hole," unpublished manuscript. Colorado History Center.

Moffat County Court records. Craig, Colorado.

Tennent, William. Personal remembrances and notes. Museum of Northwest Colorado.

Willis, Ann Bassett. Letters, notes, and personal items. Museum of Northwest Colorado.

Willis, Ann Bassett. *Scars and Two Bars*, partial memoir. Museum of Northwest Colorado. Also see *Moffat County Mirror*.

Willis, Ann Bassett. "Queen Ann of Browns Park," *Colorado Magazine* XXIX (April, January, and October 1952) and XXX (January 1953). Denver Public Library.

Willis, Frank. "Confidentially Told," unpublished manuscript. Museum of Northwest Colorado.

## Interviews and Correspondence

Davidson, Dan (director, Museum of Northwest Colorado), September 20, 2009; March 18, 2011; July 25 and 26, 2014; January 26 and 29, 2015; June 1, 2, and 3, 2015; and May 25, 2018.

DeJournette, Richard "Dick" and Daun, March 17 and 18, 1997, and April 2, 1997.

Fuller, Michelle (Uintah County Library, Vernal, Utah), August 1, 2, 3, and 6, 2016; May 22 and 25, 2018; and September 7 and 8, 2018.

Gerber, Jan (Museum of Northwest Colorado), September 12, 20, 21, and 22, 2008; June 11, 2009; April 8, 2012; January 25, 2015; June 1, 2, 3, 5, and 29, 2015; July 16 and 17, 2015; and August 13 and 14, 2015.
Hoy, Valentine IV, July 25 and 26, 2014.


## ARCHIVES AND ADDITIONAL SOURCES
Bureau of Land Management
Colorado County and Federal Census records
Dinosaur National Monument archives
Library of Congress
Uintah County Library and Museum archives
Utah Department of Community and Culture
Utah State Historical Society Research Center and Collections
United States National Archives, records of Private Amos Herbert Bassett and photo collection


## BOOKS
Athearn, Frederic J. *An Isolated Empire: A History of Northwestern Colorado*. Colorado Bureau of Land Management, 1982.
Ball, Larry D. *Tom Horn: In Life and Legend*. Norman: University of Oklahoma Press, 2014.
Burroughs, John Rolfe. *Where the Old West Stayed Young*. New York: William Morrow and Company, 1962.
Carlson, Chip. *Tom Horn: Blood on the Moon*. Glendo, WY: High Plains Press, 2001.
DeJournette, Dick and Daun. *One Hundred Years of Brown's Park and Diamond Mountain*. DeJournette Enterprises, 1996.
Ellison, Douglas W. *David Lant: The Vanished Outlaw*. Aberdeen, SD: Midstates Printing, Inc., 1988.
Ernst, Donna B. *Women of the Wild Bunch, Fort Worth Five*. Souderton, PA: Wild Bunch Press, 2004.
Ernst, Donna B., et al. *The Sundance Kid: The Life of Harry Alonzo Longabaugh*. Norman: University of Oklahoma Press, 2009.
Gulick, Bill. *Manhunt: The Pursuit of Harry Tracy*. Caldwell, ID: Caxton Press, 1999.
Horn, Tom. *Life of Tom Horn, Written by Himself*. Norman: University of Oklahoma Press, 1964.
Kouris, Diana Allen. *The Romantic and Notorious History of Browns Park*. Wolverine Gallery Publishers, 1988.
McClure, Grace. *The Bassett Women*. Athens, OH: Swallow Press, 1985.
Museum of Northwest Colorado. *Early Craig*. Mount Pleasant, SC: Arcadia Publishing, 2013.
Patterson, Richard. *Butch Cassidy: A Biography*. Lincoln: University of Nebraska Press, 1998.

Warner, Matt, et al. *Last of the Bandit Riders . . . Revisited.* Big Moon Traders, 2000.

Wommack, Linda. *From the Grave: A Roadside Guide to Colorado's Pioneer Cemeteries.* Caldwell, ID: Caxton Press, 1998.

## JOURNALS AND PERIODICALS

"Life Visits Josie, Queen of Cattle Rustlers." *Life*, January 5, 1948, 84–87.

Monaghan, Jay. Moffat County CWA Papers. Colorado History Center.

# Index of Names

# About the Author

A Colorado native, Linda Wommack is a Colorado historian and historical consultant. As an award-winning author, she has written several books on Colorado history, including *From the Grave: A Roadside Guide to Colorado's Pioneer Cemeteries, Our Ladies of the Tenderloin: Colorado's Legends in Lace, Colorado History for Kids, Colorado's Landmark Hotels, Colorado's Historic Mansions & Castles, Murder in the Mile High City* and *Haunted Cripple Creek and Teller County*. She has also contributed to two anthologies concerning Western Americana.

Linda has been a contributing editor for *True West* magazine since 1995, and a staff writer, contributing a monthly article for *Wild West* magazine, since 2004. She has also written for *The Tombstone Epitaph*, the nation's oldest continuously published newspaper, since 1993, and writes for several publications throughout her state.

Linda's research has been used in several documentary accounts for the national Wild West History Association, historical treatises of the Sand Creek Massacre, and critical historical aspects for the new Lawman & Outlaw Museum in Cripple Creek, Colorado, which opened in 2007.

Linda feeds her passion for history with activities in many local, state, and national preservation projects, by participating in historical venues (including speaking engagements), and by hosting tours, and she is involved in historical reenactments across the state.

As a longtime member of the national Western Writers of America, she has served as a judge for the acclaimed national Spur Awards in Western American literature for eight years. She is a member of both the state and national Cemetery Preservation Associations, the Gilpin

County Historical Society, and the national Wild West History Association, and she is an honorary lifetime member of the Pikes Peak Heritage Society. As a member of Women Writing the West (WWW), Linda has organized quarterly meetings for the Colorado members of WWW for the past six years and served on the 2014 WWW steering committee. She currently serves as a board member and is chair of the Women Writing the West DOWNING Journalism Award.